THE FILMS OF
NICOLAS ROEG

Neil Sinyard is a Lecturer in Literature and Film at Hull University.

He is a regular contributor to publications of the British Film Institute and writes reviews and articles for such publications as *Sight and Sound, Films and Filming, The Movie, Positif* and *Cinema Papers*. He contributes regularly to *Magill's Cinema Annual* and recently contributed to *Magill's Survey of Cinema: Foreign Language Films*.

His books include *Journey Down Sunset Boulevard: the Films of Billy Wilder, Filming Literature: the Art of Screen Adaptation, The Films of Alfred Hitchcock, The Films of Woody Allen, The Films of Steven Spielberg, The Films of Richard Lester, The Films of Mel Brooks, Classic Movies, Directors: the All-Time Greats, Marilyn, The Best of Disney* and *Silent Movies*.

THE FILMS OF
NICOLAS ROEG

NEIL SINYARD

First published in 1991
by Charles Letts & Co Ltd
Diary House, Borough Road,
London SE1 1DW

ISBN 1 85238 166 3

A CIP catalogue record for this book is available from the British Library

'Letts' is a registered trademark of Charles Letts (Scotland) Ltd

Phototypeset by Intype, London
Printed and bound in Great Britain by Butler and Tanner Ltd, Frome

Cover photograph: *Walkabout*, Jenny Agutter and David Gumpilil

All photographs used in this book were supplied by the BFI Stills, Posters and Designs Department.

Contents

Acknowledgments

There are a number of people I would like to thank for help during the writing of this book. The initial impetus for the book came from an Adult Education Course on Roeg I taught at the Triangle Cinema in Birmingham in 1985. I would like to thank the students on the course for stimulating a number of ideas; and I would particularly like to thank the Cinema Director of the Triangle, Peter Walsh for initiating the course and for consistent encouragement of the book. I am grateful to Alison Starling for her interest in the book at an earlier stage, and equally grateful to Cortina Butler at Charles Letts for nurturing it patiently and constructively to its conclusion. Many thanks are due to Carol Bucknall for the typing of my manuscript. I am indebted to the Leverhulme Trust for a research award that helped towards the completion of the book. Lastly, the book could not have been written without the support of my family, my wife Lesley, my daughter Natalie and (making their first appearance during the latter stages of the writing of the book) my twins, Jessica and Joel: the book is dedicated to them all.

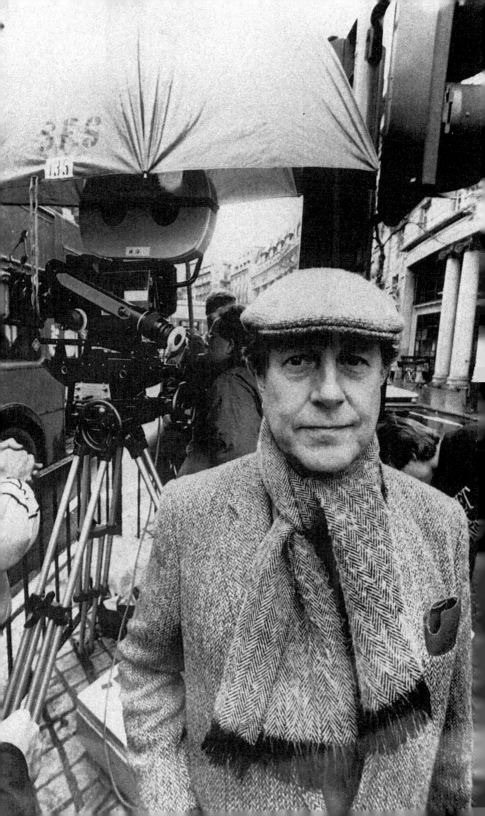

Introduction

When François Truffaut made his famous remark about the incompatibility of the terms 'cinema' and 'Britain', he certainly cannot have been thinking of Nicolas Roeg. Of course, Roeg's career as a director had not started when Truffaut made the remark: indeed, Roeg had just completed photographing Truffaut's own first film in England, *Fahrenheit 451* (1966), a movie Roeg much admired. It is tempting to speculate that Roeg might have gone into direction almost in order to prove Truffaut wrong. The most immediately striking thing about Roeg's films is the arresting visual style – bold use of slow motion, fragmented narratives, subliminal images, audacious cross-cutting, a mosaic-like use of montage, and a packed visual and aural surface that engages an audience's attention on more than one level at any time. He is a complete film-maker who, one feels, could not express himself in any other form.

Roeg is also a demanding director. He demands a lot of audiences, who have to follow complicated narratives, complex heroes and heroines and extremes of sex and violence. Roeg's films often provoke a polarity of response: some find them uncomfortable and distasteful whilst others find the films literally sensational, offering a glimpse into another world and profoundly shaking their perceptions. What then are the characteristics of his cinema that have so excited or appalled critics, exhibitors and audiences?

To return to Truffaut's comment, which he made in his book-length interview with Hitchcock: 'Isn't there a certain incompatibility between the terms "cinema" and "Britain"?'[1] When pressed by Hitchcock to define what he meant, Truffaut listed a number of British characteristics that he thought were in essence anti-cinematic: subdued emotion, unshowy visual modesty, absence of passion, literariness. Whether one agrees with that or not it makes a useful point of departure for defining the characteristics of a Nicolas Roeg film, which are in almost complete opposition to Truffaut's list of British qualities.

Take, for example, the quality of literariness: the primacy of words and of actors and actresses interpreting those words, which certainly does account for a major part of the greatness of some of the classics of British film, like *Henry V* (1944), *Brief Encounter* (1945), *The Third Man* (1949), *Kind Hearts and Coronets* (1949), *The French Lieutenant's Woman* (1981), and many others. To contrast Roeg's films with these is not to denigrate either but to suggest that they belong to a different tradition of British film. Roeg's films are thought out completely in cinematic terms and the script is merely a guide, a blueprint, a catalyst. 'The screenwriter can't *complete* his job', Roeg has said, 'it's the film itself that will complete his job.'[2] Two stories about the scripts of *Performance* and *Walkabout* perhaps illustrate the point best. Roeg and his co-director on *Performance*, Donald Cammell, were highly amused when visited by a worried Warner Brothers executive who had been flown out to stop the film because they were not sticking to the script. 'Show us where we're straying,' they asked him, and naturally he could not because there never *was* a final script. On *Walkabout*, Roeg had left the writer Edward Bond for eight weeks while he scouted for locations and when he returned and asked Bond how he had got on, he was handed fourteen pages of handwritten notes, with the accompanying comment, 'I think it's rather good.' Many directors might have been thrown or even annoyed by this. Roeg's reaction? 'They were *exactly* what I wanted,' he said. It was something on which his imagination could build.

Roeg's films are so cinematic that they are inconceivable in any other form. They are not verbally paraphrasable: a published screenplay would hardly make sense on its own. They are cripplingly diminished on video. Until its recent showing on British television,

Eureka had probably been seen by more people on video than on the cinema screen, for its distribution was limited. 'It's useful as a reference', says Roeg, 'but the scale of it is all wrong – the whole point of the film is these are *big* characters . . . the gangster is supposed to be *terrifying*.'[3] Also Roeg's films have sometimes proved too hot to handle on television. *Don't Look Now* was stripped of its love scene when first shown on British television: the BBC screened the re-edited, truncated American version (the full scene was restored in Roeg's cut for its next TV showing, after public pressure). For a long time, *Bad Timing* was only available to British television in a 'specially re-edited version' which so diminished the film that it was turned down by the BBC's Films Acquisition Officer, Brian Baxter. (It was finally shown on Channel 4, ten years after its release.)

This raises a related point, which also runs contrary to Truffaut's view of the British. Far from being emotionally subdued, Roeg's cinema is extremely passionate, extremely sexy. He is the most Freudian and the most Lawrentian of modern directors. Bourgeois civilization is stifling, neurosis-inducing, the films either imply or state: man and woman need to rediscover the vitality of their original nature (a theme set out in its most primitive, almost diagrammatic form in *Castaway*). Emotions in Roeg's work oscillate violently between extremes of love and hate and go quite beyond British cinema's traditional three Rs: rationalism, realism, restraint. Roeg's world is more commonly the opposite of that: irrational, surreal, unrestrained. His films are wild, dream-like, powerfully erotic. They are (to redeploy an outmoded phrase) mind-blowing – almost literally, for many characters in Roeg do lose their heads or put bullets through their brains. The extreme reactions they induce are comparable, in terms of British cinema, only to the outcries that greeted Michael Powell after *Peeping Tom* (1959) or Ken Russell after *The Devils* (1971). *Eureka* must be unique in that it was hated so much by the distributors that it was not allowed to be shown even in cinemas that wanted it. 'We're rethinking the release pattern,' Roeg was told, and discovered that there were only two copies of the film, which the distributors would release only if Roeg agreed to tour round with it and talk about it afterwards. (Much to Roeg's amazement, when he agreed to do this, the distributors even checked up that he did actually attend the few screenings.)

So Roeg's cinema is exactly what Truffaut said British cinema was not: totally cinematic and unliterary, uninhibited, passionate and extreme. The films are 'difficult' – to follow, to assimilate, to take, sometimes. The casts are weird. Pop stars like Mick Jagger, David Bowie and Art Garfunkel are used in bizarre contexts, and as Rip Torn said about his co-starring with Bowie, Buck Henry and Candy Clark in *The Man Who Fell to Earth*: 'I don't know whether it's a cast for a movie but it would make a hell of a dinner party.' The films are often horrific. Roeg belongs to the 'mad poet' stream of British cinema which, for some, is the real, great tradition of British film: not the tasteful quality cinema of Lean, Olivier, Carol Reed, the social realists, Puttnam or Attenborough, but the cinema of Powell and Pressburger, Russell, Boorman, Michael Reeves – Hammer rather than Ealing. Roeg's films are not naturalistic but abnormal, extraordinary mental, psychological structures that reflect the psyches of characters who are deeply alone, whose bodies are in one place but whose minds are in another. His films are rarely simple linear structures. There is a very original treatment of time in them, consisting of odd jumps, tiny events, nothing, something ordinary, suddenly something crucial that comes out of nowhere and hits you. They are stream-of-thought films that seem to gather a late-night cult following, as if, like Joyce's *Finnegan's Wake*, they function best in that mysterious free-ranging mental area between the waking and the dreaming state. They are films that attempt to push beyond the natural, rational world (like Expressionism, Surrealism, like Schiele in painting, like Borges or Marquez in fiction). They are films that sometimes, in a way, are glimpses of the infinite, searches for Eureka.

'The film belongs to the spectator as much as to the

4

director,' Roeg says, 'even more so.' His films are open structures which make an audience work and think. 'Filmgoers have been conditioned,' he says, contemplating the resistance to some of his work. 'They expect the same sort of answers in a film: What's the plot? What happens here? What comes next? I get very frustrated. But to be bitter about people not liking you – that would be a very spoilt attitude. It's like trying to force food on someone. That's something I admire very much in Welles – he never became bitter no matter what people said.'[4] Roeg's attitude, he says, is the following: 'All you're doing in a film really is saying: this is what, and how, I think – is there anybody out there?'[5]

The basic situation of a Roeg film is nearly always the same. The leading character is thrust into a strange milieu to which he or she must adjust or from which he or she must struggle free – what Roeg describes as a 'study of what can happen when you step out of your moral background, out of where you are in life.' *Performance* acts like a hallucinatory drug; *Walkabout* is a sensual rite of passage; *Don't Look Now* gives us all second sight; *The Man Who Fell to Earth* projects us into an alien vision of fallen modern man. James Fox in *Performance*, Jenny Agutter in *Walkabout*, Donald Sutherland in *Don't Look Now*, Art Garfunkel in *Bad Timing* are all relatively conservative, emotionally vulnerable people who are suddenly given a glimpse of a more exciting, yet more dangerous world, that puts passion above reason, instinct above intelligence. To pursue this vision could lead to emotional liberation, self-knowledge or, alternatively, madness. Not to pursue it, and stay where you are in life, could result in safety, security but also sterility, frustration, emotional repression. This is the challenge: this is the danger.

Nicolas Roeg was born in London on 15 August, 1928. His interest in film began at school where he attempted to run a film society, and it continued during his service in the army where he was unit projectionist. After the Second World War, he got a job in the film industry, as clapper boy, then tea-maker, and then camera assistant. The first lesson he was given, he says, came from the experienced Hollywood cameraman, Joseph Ruttenberg, who was photographing *The Miniver Story* (1950) in England. When Roeg asked him what he was doing, Ruttenberg replied that he was aiming for 'images that create the mood for the story'. It was a lesson Roeg took to heart. He was also part of the camera crew on such films as *Ivanhoe* (1952), *The Adventures of Quentin Durward* (1955), *Bhowani Junction* (1956) and *Tarzan's Greatest Adventure* (1959), the latter featuring a young Sean Connery as the villain. He also worked as a camera operator on Fred Zinnemann's Australian film *The Sundowners* (1960); he worked on the second unit for the train crash sequence of David Lean's *Lawrence of Arabia* (1962); and he wrote the story for a Stanley Baker thriller, *A Prize of Arms* (1961), directed by Cliff Owen, about a plot to rob an Army payroll. Finally he graduated to become a director of photography. Among the major films he photographed in the 1960s were *The Caretaker* (1963) and *Nothing but the Best* (1964) for director Clive Donner; *The Masque of the Red Death* (1964) for Roger Corman; *Fahrenheit 451* (1966) for François Truffaut; *Far from the Madding Crowd* (1967) for John Schlesinger; and *A Funny Thing Happened on the Way to the Forum* (1966) and *Petulia* (1968) for Richard Lester.

Roeg is sometimes reluctant to talk about his early career as cinematographer ('Oh God, must we?' he said to one interviewer. 'I'd rather not!'[6]) It is possible that he feels he accepted too many uncongenial assignments: not even his photography could give much interest to James Hill's *Every Day's a Holiday* (1964) or Michael Winner's *The System* (1964). Perhaps he dates his real emergence on the film scene from his career as a director. Yet clearly the experience was valuable training, enabling him to watch directors closely: to see, for example, how Cukor worked with actors (*Bhowani Junction*), how Corman inspired a film crew, how Truffaut worked out the look of a film.

Indeed, his work as a cameraman has intriguing hints of his forthcoming work as a director. Corman's *The Masque of the Red Death* not only anticipates the kind of horror imagery that will become a feature of Roeg's work; its actual 'Red Death' figure will recur in a different guise in Roeg's *Don't Look Now*. Richard Lester's masterpiece *Petulia*, enhanced by Roeg's brilliant camerawork, not only anticipates the kind of splintered narrative and complex time jumps that crop up in Roeg's work: the film's theme of the disintegration of 60s permissiveness into despair and violence in 'flower power' America will be echoed in a British context in Roeg's directorial debut, *Performance* (co-directed with Donald Cammell). And Roeg's later film, *Bad Timing* also seems to owe a lot to *Petulia* (its title even derives from a dialogue exchange between George C. Scott and Julie Christie in Lester's film). Both *Bad Timing* and *Petulia* have the hospital as an important central image and a grisly motif of surgical dissection that serves as a metaphor for self and social laceration. Both films deal with an ultimately doomed romance between a deceptively liberated heroine and a disturbingly inhibited older man in a context of socio-sexual dislocation.

Although *A Funny Thing Happened on the Way to the Forum* does not connect so obviously with Roeg's future directing development, the photography is nevertheless striking: odd splashes of colour, variation between the painted interiors and the crisp reality of the exteriors, the odd surreal shot (a male quartet prancing on an aqueduct as they sing 'Everybody ought to have a maid'). If editing, as Lester says, is evidence of the director's metabolism and the way his mind works, then one might say that Roeg's editing in his films is evidence of his lateral thinking.

Roeg's photography in the 1960s was very distinctive, and attracted much critical attention. In some cases it was closely controlled by the director. Roeg has paid tribute to the whole visual conception of Truffaut's grossly undervalued sci-fi classic *Fahrenheit 451*, to the way its glossy, cold, futuristic surface blandness eloquently reflects a world where feelings and language have been flattened into banal conformity. 'That film had a tremendous influence on cinema, as well as on me', said Roeg. 'François is a very great man of the cinema.'[7] Roeg's own sci-fi classic *The Man Who Fell to Earth* shows that influence, similarly exposing the terrifying emptiness of modern life through the perspective of an alien yet penetrating vision.

In other cases, Roeg's photography had the effect of making some directors look more stylish than they perhaps deserved. Subtract Roeg from the career of Clive Donner (he photographed *The Caretaker* and *Nothing but the Best* for him) and you are not left with a lot. Roeg's photography of *Far from the Madding Crowd* – his endeavour 'to get the very feel of Hardy's countryside on the screen', as he put it – has rightly always been the most acclaimed aspect of an otherwise lumpish and dull film.

What is unusual about the nature of Roeg's transformation from cameraman to director? Simply this. A number of fine British cameramen, like Ronald Neame (*Pygmalion*), Guy Green (*Great Expectations*), Jack Cardiff (*Black Narcissus*) and Freddie Francis (*Sons and Lovers, The Elephant Man, Glory*) have become directors. But when they have turned to direction, not one has shown the visual stylishness that characterized their photographic work: they have, for the most part, made visually dull, plodding, uninteresting movies. By contrast, Roeg has gone into direction and, from the beginning, has directed films that have as much visual impact as those films he photographed. The first example of this, and a sensational one, was *Performance*.

The Films

Performance
(1970)

Sub-standard crime meller with sadism and sex hypes. Dull b.o. outlook. For the psyched set.

(Variety)[1]

Dense Pinterish melodrama about alter egos; not really worth the trouble it takes, but superficially very flashily done.

(Leslie Halliwell)[2]

Performance was finally shown to the British public in January 1971, its screening having been held up for three years because of the film's so-called 'excessive violence'. The delay could have been disastrous, because the film is crucially about the end of the 1960s and could have seemed dated by the time it finally opened. However, the style was perceived as being advanced even in the 1970s, so that, when the film was reissued in 1977, it came with the advertising slogan: 'Ten years ahead of its time . . . are you now ready for *Performance?*' It was a film that undoubtedly threw down a gauntlet to traditional British cinema of the period, in the same way that Michael Powell's *Peeping Tom* had done a decade earlier. Even now the absence of consensus over *Performance* can be seen in the widely different responses to it in several standard histories of British film.[3]

It is a rare bird in British cinema: a major Modernist movie. It anticipates Roeg's future work in all kinds of ways: in his casting of a pop star – Mick Jagger – in a

James Fox, Mick Jagger

11

leading role (compare the casting of David Bowie in *The Man Who Fell to Earth* and Art Garfunkel in *Bad Timing*); in the movie's exploration of the theme of identity, a pressing Roeg concern; in the film's gangster milieu, an environment which is also glimpsed in *The Man Who Fell to Earth*, *Eureka* and *Insignificance*. The most significant way it points to the future is through its style, which is dense and daring.

Nothing could be simpler than the basic plot. A flashy young gangster called Chas (played by James Fox) has to go on the run when he antagonizes his boss, Flowers (Johnny Shannon), by murdering a rival, Joey (Anthony Valentine), in a grudge vendetta. He eventually hides out in a house run by a reclusive pop star in retirement, Turner (Mick Jagger), who has two young ladies, Pherber (Anita Pallenberg) and Lucy (Michelle Breton), also in attendance. They begin to put pressure on Chas, feeding him drugs and breaking down his sense of identity. The climax is violent.

Yet the film's approach towards its narrative is oblique. The story never seems 'foregrounded'; the film does not invite you to identify or sympathize overtly with a star actor of character; it does not pretend to be a 'realistic' film with 'well-rounded' characters in any traditional sense. Instead it invites you to follow not so much a linear plot as a cluster of themes and structured juxtapositions: life/death; male/female; sanity/insanity; reality/performance; wholeness of personality/disintegration of identity.

For some, at the time of its appearance, it seemed insufferably self-indulgent and pretentious, though not many went as far as John Simon: 'You don't have to be a drug addict, pederast, sado-masochist or nitwit to enjoy it, but being one or more of these things would help.'[4] For others it was and remains a milestone of British movie-making, experimental, challenging and subversive. It is an art movie aimed at a youth audience, something that Francis Ford Coppola was to attempt years later in *Rumble Fish* (1983). In contrast to the predominantly conservative forms of 1960s British film, its time-leaps and enigmatic narrative seemed redolent of the cinematic experimentation of contemporary masters such as Alain Resnais, Michelangelo Antonioni and Jean-Luc Godard.

Three artistic parallels immediately suggest themselves. It is a film that courts comparison with Ingmar Bergman's masterpiece *Persona* (1966) which, incidentally, would serve as an equally good title for *Performance*. Like *Persona*, Roeg's film is about the interaction and struggle for psychological dominance between two personalities, one an imaginative artist, the other a more mundane character whose world of reality the artist subtly begins to subvert. There are also visual similarities, at the moments when the faces of the two main characters in each film merge or melt into one another. Each movie makes use of a similar narrative fragmentation, which seems to be in part the product of a context of social violence. Both are modernist texts that revel in being difficult, in announcing that realism has had its day. They are films that rejoice in streams of consciousness (like Joyce), reject the arid observation of everyday trivialities and destroy the old stable ego of character. If the literary shadow behind *Persona* is Strindberg, the literary shadow behind *Performance* is perhaps Borges. It reflects a world that is surrealist and labyrinthine, an age of experimentation (social, sexual, artistic) that is now close to exhaustion.

A second comparison that suggests itself is with Harold Pinter. Like so much of Pinter, the basic setting of the film is a house or room, and the basic situation is that of an intruder whose appearance throws the previous power relationships into chaos. The gangster background of *Performance*, with its mixture of Cockney mirth and menace, is reminiscent of the Pinteresque world of *The Dumb Waiter* and *The Homecoming*; and the ping-pong verbal exchanges between Chas and Turner display a combination of comedy and tension worthy of Pinter at his best. (Amidst the visual pyrotechnics, one should not overlook the fact that *Performance* seems a brilliantly written film, though in the absence of a completed screenplay, it may be that much of the credit should go to the improvizational skills of the actors.) In this context, it is worth remembering that Roeg was the cameraman on Clive Donner's fine film version of Pinter's *The Caretaker*, a possible influence. It is also worth mentioning that *Performance* has much in common with a contemporary film by Pinter's favourite director of this time, *Secret Ceremony* (1968) by Joseph Losey. Losey's film looks, in a way, like a feminine version of *Performance*, likewise exploring an enigmatic interchange of personalities (wigs and mirrors similarly prominent in the imagery) that will culminate in murder. Both films make Britain look fundamentally strange; each uses a green filter at times to give a sickly weirdness to the images. To cap this similarity of theme and style, both films are set in houses in Notting Hill, London, about two hundred yards from each other.

A final comparison might be made with Richard Lester's 1968 masterpiece, *Petulia*, which Roeg so stunningly photographed, and which anatomized a 60s society in its death throes. Like *Petulia*, *Performance* leaps about in time and space, as it exposes an era of permissiveness now collapsing under the twin onslaughts of drugs and violence. It was in this context that *Performance* had most relevance at the time of its making. Its cinema of violent fantasy did indeed have a particular excitement for a younger generation, and its imaginative poetry more than any empirical naturalism seemed to make the European avant garde rather than the British New Wave its natural soul mates. But, fundamentally, *Performance* is cinema of disintegration, reflecting uncertainties not only in the old stable narrative-character type of story-telling but in society itself. 'The drug thing', says Roeg, 'was not bound in merely with the story; it was also that at the time (and of course *Performance* was released in England a year after it was completed) we . . . wanted something that was happening socially. The film would have been less pop, it would have been less socially accurate without the drug element and the wide boy inside the de-Quincey like attitude. I don't think it would have had its social contact.'[5]

Like *Petulia*, *Performance* is one of the great films of, and about, the late 1960s. It belongs to the pessimistic branch of permissiveness, having a late 60s anger that recognizes that the decade's early promise of freedom and egalitarianism has completely disintegrated. It is as apocalyptic in tone as Jean-Luc Godard's *Weekend* (1967). However, its cynicism and despair about the new climate find expression in a variety of ways.

To begin with, it insists on a link between the business world and the criminal underworld, in which capitalism is nourished by intimidation and protection rackets. Harry Flowers is as threatening in his world as Lee J. Cobb's dockside boss, Johnny Friendly in *On the Waterfront* (1954) was in his, but he also has a respectable front and is destined for a knighthood. (The film anticipates *The Godfather* in its oscillation between crime as big business and big business as crime.) Behind this is the well-documented terrorization of the East End in the 1960s by the Kray Twins, who also had a respectable front and links with both the business world and showbiz, organizing American boxing tournaments for charity, and entertaining personalities like Barbara Windsor and Jackie Collins in their club, the Double R. Some of Ronnie Kray's comments ('I like conservative clothes. I can't stand anybody flash') and traits (uninterested in women but wary of homosexuality) might well have furnished the inspiration for the character of Chas in *Performance*.

Britain is a decadent society in *Performance*, in which the young are either disillusioned or disaffected. It would not be too fanciful to see *Performance* as an allegory about the legacy of Harold Wilson's government, with its betrayal of its promises of 'revolution' (promises rendered worthless by devaluation, by the accommodation and appropriation of youth culture – the Beatles become Members of the British Empire – and by its unpopular obeisance to American policy in Vietnam). After the protest and idealism, power still lay in the hands of the political gangster: the young, as John Lennon said, had been betrayed. Betrayal is a key theme in *Performance*.

Turner's flat is decorated with figures of great potential who betrayed their promise or who died in violent circumstances (James Dean, Martin Luther King). The Swingin' Britain of Richard Lester's *A Hard Day's Night* (1964) has mutated in *Performance* into a satanic nightmare where Turner is driven into exile when he catches a glimpse of his own demon in the mirror, where he is terrified by his self-image. The film's use of Mick Jagger as a symbol of rebellious counter-culture, with associations of Satanism, violence, deviant sexuality, adds an extra explosive dimension. More than the Beatles, Jagger symbolizes *alienated* youth. More even than that, Jagger seems alienated by his own image.

Nevertheless, *Performance* cannot be tied exclusively to its period (as its reissue in 1977 – 'now you're almost ready for *Performance* . . . ' indicates). Three things undoubtedly assisted its reputation in the period between its making and its reissue. First, its violence had anticipated many subsequent developments in modern cinema across a wide spectrum of genres, from the Western (pre-eminently, *The Wild Bunch* in 1969) to the horror musical (*Phantom of the Paradise* in 1974): it no longer looked so strange in 1977, in a cinema era in which violence had been taken to the point of rhapsodic sensuality. Also, the violence of its visual stylization and weird characterization now perhaps looked less extreme after the disturbing impact of *A Clockwork Orange* (1971). Secondly, the film had certainly become more assimilable as the profile of Roeg himself as a director became clearer. Thirdly, the reputation of the film had probably been assisted by certain developments in film studies and theory, where critical ideas now centred less on 'morality' and 'significance' than on 'structure' and 'signification': less on *what* something means than on *how* it means. *Performance* had become an especially interesting text because of its complexity and density, because of its denial of easy character identification, and because it lent itself to being read not so much in terms of linear narrative as in terms of inner structure.

To make a simple point about structure in *Performance*: it is clear that the film breaks into two distinct halves; one can read this split in a variety of ways. The structural division, or duality, mirrors the stark contrast between the two main characters, particularly in the image they project of maleness. Chas (Fox) is a traditional conservative male – macho, hard, obsessed with personal appearance, tidy, and with his feet in the real world. This is the image he projects, and sees, of himself. By contrast, Turner (Jagger) is deviant, sensual, bisexual and a counter-culture opposition to Chas's conservatism. The two, in other words, are so sharply divided, as almost to belong to different worlds, or different films: *this* film will throw them violently together.

The structural dualism also mirrors the film's play with two different kinds of narrative, in which the overall linear progression of the first part (and for all the complexity of the montage, it does tell the story of Chas's straight-line course towards destruction) gives way to the liquidity of the second, where time seems almost to stand still as identity shifts. The two-part structure also mirrors the film's theme of split personality.

Performance can finally be read as a two-part study not only of identity but of power. The first part is concerned with political, social, physical power, and its attendant qualities: wealth, influence, fear, brutality, torture and intimidation. The second part is concerned with psychological power, the power not of getting inside someone's house but of getting inside someone's head. The key to the doors of perception is drugs, and the insights that are revealed lead not to fear of external violence but to inner uncertainty, and the question: 'Who am I?'

The first part of *Performance* establishes both the character of Chas and his milieu. At the outset he is self-confident, cocky, sure of his identity. When he is growing overly aggressive towards the bookie Joey Maddox (Anthony Valentine) and Flowers demands, 'Who do you think you are?' Chas replies quietly: 'I know who I am, Harry.' His flat is an extension of that ostensible certainty and control: bare and tidy – at one stage, he briefly tidies the magazines on a table – in a way that perhaps duplicates his straightforward, limited outlook on life. It certainly is a complete contrast to the chaos and confusion of Turner's room. Yet, in retrospect, this opening is significant in discreetly suggesting certain fissures beginning to appear in Chas's character and to undermine his self-satisfaction. He might know who he is, but to others, he is 'Jack the Lad', 'The Lone Ranger'. His constant inspection of himself in a mirror goes beyond narcissism: it seems to suggest a subconscious anxiety over identity, a sense of the fragility and possible fragmentation of identity. Also, his hatred of Joey, who used to be his friend ('Let me see to the ponce, putting the frighteners on flash little twerps . . . ' he says) has an intensity bordering on obsession. Might Joey be a dimension of Chas's repressed homosexuality that must be violently rejected? The word 'Ponce' is daubed on the wall of Chas's flat when Maddox and his gang break in and beat him up. The previously spick-and-span flat, now turned upside down in an orgy of blood, paint and filth, serves as a correlative to the change that will take place in Chas when he encounters Turner in the second half of the film.[6] Like so many of Roeg's heroes, he will be suddenly thrust into an alien world in which his framework of values will be upended and assailed.

Chas is one of the protection boys of Harry Flowers, a gangster who maintains a façade of respectability and has strong links with the City and commerce. Chas's violent opening progress is cross-cut with a court case in which a barrister (Allan Cuthbertson) representing a business rival of Harry's – the lawyer's chauffeur will be brutally assaulted and his head shaved when his master fails to be warned off – is making a distinction between 'merger' and 'takeover'. Both are euphemisms, since what is involved here is less partnership than intimidation: for Flowers, the line between the methods of the businessman and the gangster is non-existent. Merger or takeover means physical violence. (In the second half of the film, this theme will also be taken up but with a shift of emphasis: the theme there will be *psychological* mergers and takeovers.)

The dramatic climax of the first half of the film is the confrontation between Chas, Flowers and Joey Maddox after the latter's betting shop has been raided and looted as a warning to keep up his protection payments. There is a scintillating pointillism of detail here, through the intercutting, the use of counterpoint and the sharp rhythms of Jack Nitzsche's superb score: subliminal shots of the house, the smashing up of Maddox's shop, a split-second glimpse of him as a boxer, his profession before his present trade. At one moment, Roeg fades the image to black-and-white and Flowers diminishes before our eyes, as if representing Chas's wish to cut him down to size. This jolting of conventional perception is a premonition of what will happen to Chas later in the film, just as Roeg's almost imperceptible shift from the jury at a trial to an audience at a porno film (are they the same people and, if so, what kind of 'judges' are they?) is also preparing for a dramatic shift in context in Chas's life – a shift into an environment where he will wonder where he is, in his life, in his head. The whole scene is important for later developments, because it will form the basis of Chas's later hallucinations after taking drugs, when Turner (the new 'boss' in Chas's life) takes the role of Flowers in Chas's imagination and the men have to dance to his tune in 'Memo to Turner'. Also crucial lines in the film ('I've known a few performers in my time . . . ', 'He enjoys his work . . . ', 'You push the buttons . . . ', 'An out-of-date boy . . . ') first occur here and are to return with a different force and feeling.

The narrative turning point of the film is Chas's murder of Maddox, after the latter and his friends have invaded Chas's flat and violently beaten him up. As in Pinter, this invasion of space is felt as a violation of person, and Chas's orderly life, surroundings and personality have suddenly been put under siege. The lurking fear of homosexuality is pushed disturbingly close to the surface. 'Why don't you give him the kiss of life, Joey?' sneers one of Maddox's henchmen as Chas lies helpless ('Shut your filthy mouth!' is Maddox's perhaps too vehement reply). But Chas regains the initiative when he manages to pull a gun, and his words before shooting Maddox, 'I am a bullet,' are a reaffirmation of self after a savage struggle.

The killing is an act that draws Chas's associates into a criminal and embarrassing situation (warning Chas off from harassing Maddox, Flowers has cautioned Chas, 'At the death, who's left holding the sodding baby?') and, in a double-chase situation out of Hitchcock, Chas has to flee both the law and Flowers' henchmen. He dyes his hair red (Turner is painting his flat red at the same time, a premonitory connection between the two). He rings his mother, doodling a sketch of a hanged man at the same time and checking his transformed appearance in the mirror of the phone booth, and then by chance overhears a conversation in a railway cafe about a vacancy in Turner's apartment. He goes to inspect, and the texture and tempo of the film change.

Pretending to Turner that he is 'a juggler . . . an artist like yourself', Chas tries to persuade him to let him have the flat. 'If you were me, what would you do?' asks Turner. The seeds for an exchange of personality are being sown. Although some of the lines of the early part of the film begin to recur in the second ('you enjoy your work', 'pushing the buttons'), they now seem a distant recollection of a far-off land: the context is so changed. Whilst Chas's identity seemed fairly static in the first part of the film, he now goes through numerous changes of image and costume, partly because of the need for disguise and concealment (he is secretly making arrangements to obtain a passport photograph and get out of the country), but also precipitated by the disorienting impact on him of Turner and his two girlfriends.

Whereas the style in the first part of the film was hard and staccato, it now is more fluid and languorous. Faces dissolve into each other and sometimes a back is more revealing than a face.[7] Male and female blend, and words too become blurred and ambiguous, as the dialogue puns on the words 'dyed' and 'died', 'shot' (medicinal) and 'shot' (gun). Turner has a guitar solo that is loose and improvisational and sets the scene;

Chas, who has hitherto dictated the pace, has to adjust to a new dance of death. Perceptions change. Through the drugs he has been fed by Turner and Pherber, Chas begins to see all kinds of different perspectives on Turner's table. 'How much do you want for this, *Turn*?' he asks; the significance of the pop star's name is revealed – Turner is now turning the tables on his guest. The blurring of edges, where different identities and realities seem to melt and merge, is enhanced by the casting of Mick Jagger who is, and is not, playing himself and who, like the characters in Roeg's later film *Insignificance*, seems to stand somewhere between real-life personality and fictional persona.

'We have to go much further . . . see how you function . . . ' As the drugs take a deeper grip on Chas, Turner penetrates farther and farther beneath the surface. Turner is now in charge of Chas's mind – in Chas's fantasy Turner takes the role of Flowers. And as Chas's mental defences crumble, so we learn more about the reasons for Turner's seclusion. He has hidden himself away from the world because a vision of his demon in the mirror once frightened him by its evil (the analogy in Jagger's career was the Hells' Angels murder at a Rolling Stones concert: Don McLean's eight-minute pop song, 'American Pie', characterizes Jagger as a 'Satan laughing with delight'). What Turner sees in Chas's violence is perhaps an image of the power he once had, over audiences. 'Nothing is true, everything is permitted,' says Turner, sounding now like a spokesman for an age of permissiveness that has moved from freedom to anarchy. 'The only performance that makes it', he cries, 'that *really* makes it, that makes it all the way, is the one that achieves madness . . . ' It is an attempt to break down Chas's personality defences, perhaps to acknowledge a femaleness under the maleness, a tenderness under the terror. The performance that really makes it is the one that lets go, travels beyond inhibition and restraint, reaches into the depths of the soul, confronts but also challenges the abyss. The statement is a kind of credo for the extremes of Roeg's cinema, and for the risk-taking excesses of a

21

particular, rich strand of 'mad' British cinema.

When Chas is recaptured by the Flowers gang, it signifies the end of his inner exploration, which in turn involves the destruction of his alter ego, Turner. He becomes a bullet again, once again blowing away the mind of someone who threatens his identity, the bullet exploding the psychedelic labyrinths that have lurked within Turner and that Chas has begun to explore. (The face of the writer Borges, the magic realist who at the time was the writer opening up the corridors of the mind of disaffected youth, is summoned up here at the end of the bullet's journey.) But maybe the kind of mind-blowing exploration experienced by Chas cannot be dismissed that easily, with that brutal finality. Can he really be unchanged after his mental examination in that house, where time has seemed to stand still but where identity and integrated personality have seemed to float in constant flux? Roeg and his co-director Donald Cammell leave us in doubt: a figure is led to the gangsters' car and greeted as Chas, but the face that turns to look out of the window is Turner's.

There cannot have been many more arresting debuts in British cinema than Roeg's in *Performance*, though it is worth stressing that, in interviews, he has always insisted on its being a fifty-fifty collaboration with Donald Cammell.[8] It is a film about identity and power, but one which conveys its ideas with uncommon violence and an extraordinary richness of imagery and obliqueness of narrative. More even than *Peeping Tom*, it is the British cinema's ultimate Modernist film. Like the Modernists, it is difficult, inaccessible, refusing to pander to the common consumer; it is unafraid of affronting its audience through bad taste and rebels against traditional standards of morality. Also, like the Modernists, it is restless, dynamic, unpredictable, more interested in posing questions than supplying answers: it goes for the deep (psychological) more than the broad social canvas; and has an ending that is an enigma more than a closure. It has the century's feeling of apocalypse, of 'a coming universal wish not to live', of things 'falling apart; the centre cannot hold'; and, as a Modernist artist, Roeg conveys in *Performance*, as in nearly all of his films, a sense that the only reality is human consciousness. Like most Modernists Roeg believes in authentic response more than objective law, in the artist's need to discover his own inner demon, to experiment, to search for magic in art more than meaning, and to place less emphasis on aesthetic unity than on what Irvin Howe calls 'jagged, fragmented expressiveness' (in his book, *The Decline of the New*). It involves, as D.H. Lawrence said, a new mode of thinking, a new attitude to time. 'To appreciate the pagan manner of thought,' says Lawrence, 'we have to drop our own manner of on-and-on, from a start to a finish, and allow the mind to move in cycles, or to flit here and there over a cluster of images. Our idea of time as a continuity in an eternal straight line has crippled our consciousness cruelly.'[9] The mind moving in cycles, flitting here and there over a cluster of images: it is a wonderful picture of Roeg's method of montage.

There is another link between Roeg and Modernism, though one which throws lingering doubt over *Performance*. The Modernists were progressive formally and structurally but, more often than not, they were reactionary in politics (think of the overtones of some of the poems of Yeats, Eliot and Pound). Perhaps this is not surprising, an inevitable consequence of the artist's turning his back on society in barely disguised contempt and of his celebrating individual potency over communal responsibility. Although it might have outraged traditional moralists in its style, the attitude of *Performance* to the 'swingin'', permissive, decadent 60s seems deeply critical, even excessively so, implying a sleight-of-hand link between the criminal world and the pop world which, for example, deeply offended a champion of the liberating effect of popular culture like George Melly. The politics of Roeg's film universe proves to be a slippery subject, as a surprisingly conservative theme is sometimes teased out from what looks like a trail-blazing, mind-blowing, barrier-breaking style. As in Eliot's *The Waste Land*, the fragmentation (shored against the artist's ruins) seems to reflect less a crisis of society, though that is important, than a more fundamental crisis of identity.

Walkabout
(1970)

The three children stood looking at each other in the middle of the Australian desert. Motionless as the outcrops of granite they stared, and stared, and stared. Between them the distance was less than the spread of an outstretched arm, but more than a hundred thousand years.

(James Vance Marshall, *Walkabout*[1])

I've got a lot of children, and I've been tremendously conscious each time of this question of identity and destiny. It wasn't the visual side of the book at all. It was that here were two people – two people in effect, since the little boy really acts as a chorus to the aborigine and the girl – who by this curious moment of fate were at a point where they could have been in love with each other. They had everything to offer each other, but they couldn't communicate and went zooming to their own separate destinies, through the odd placement of identity, the identity that other people had put on them. The girl came nearly to the point where she could have changed, but then in one moment when they see the road she slipped all the way back, tumbled back into this mould. So nearly . . . and there was still doubt in her right at the end of the film.

(Nicolas Roeg[2])

Walkabout was originally to have been made before *Performance*. Roeg had scouted all the locations in Australia, no doubt drawing on observations made when he was camera operator on *The Sundowners*, and then

Lucien John, Jenny Agutter

had twenty-five copies done of the screenplay, which were sent out without success until he had only one left. 'I was reluctant to get another batch made,' he said. 'The first had cost about a hundred pounds, a lot of money to me then. Then I was advised to give it to a financier – Max Raab. On the day he was leaving London I was rung at about eight to ask whether I'd delivered it. He was leaving the Dorchester at ten. I didn't want to but did so anyway. My last copy. And by the time he'd got to New York he'd decided. And we had a financier.'[3]

Walkabout has had something of a variable critical reputation. Neil Feineman, author of a book on Roeg, says he has 'never been able to muster up more than an intellectual tolerance for *Walkabout*', and discusses it as a sentimentalized version of the Noble Savage theme.[4] On the other hand, both Basil Wright[5] and John Izod[6], for example, in impressive analyses seem to find it Roeg's most accessible and affecting film (at the time of their writing), almost a religious parable and a childhood film on a par with its near-contemporary classic, François Truffaut's *L'Enfant Sauvage* (1969). If it lacks the density of Roeg at his best, it is certainly a photographic *tour de force* and perhaps still his most moving, humane film.

The film's lack of immediate commercial success – it has since acquired something of a cult following – is probably attributable to the different levels at which it operates, and the consequent uncertainty of the distributors about which market to aim at. It is, on one level, a children's adventure film, about a girl and a boy (Jenny Agutter and Lucien John, actually Roeg's son) who are lost in the Australian desert and are rescued by an Aborigine (David Gumpilil) on his walkabout. Even here, though, there are intricate sub-divisions of style. The film pursues at times a relatively straightforward linear narrative that is nevertheless punctuated by images that are *thematically* analogous or associative rather than simple flashbacks; whilst, at certain moments, it seems like a wonderfully photographed documentary (perhaps this explains Basil Wright's admiration) of a living desert populated by

Disneyesque monsters and seeming anything but deserted. On yet another level, it is an adult film, treating mature and serious themes – innocence and experience, sexual repression, environment and ecology – in a complex, sometimes violent way. Roeg was disappointed that the film was given an 'AA' certificate in Britain, which effectively excluded the younger audience he had hoped for. 'I showed the film to a class of seven- and eight-year-olds', he said, 'who didn't have any worry or fears about certain aspects of it because they hadn't that in their experience, and so they overlooked it. And I had tried to construct *Walkabout* in such a way that children could enjoy it on the level that was designed for them, while adults would appreciate it on another level . . . I'm interested in the split senses, in engaging people's attention on more than one surface at a given time. There'll be more of this in the coming generations. Already people watch television and read a magazine at the same time, looking from one to the other. Kids are accustomed to doing two or three things at a time now. This is what I was trying to put into *Walkabout*.'[7]

Certainly, different levels of appeal and response seem part and parcel of the film's style, as it strives to convey something of the muddle and texture of modern life. The musical soundtrack has brief blasts of Stockhausen in aural contention with a John Barry score in his *Born Free* mode, whilst the radio emits snippets of programmes. Roeg's montage jumps between different events to catch odd connections between them. The children and the Aborigine play and climb a tree, a scene which is cross-cut with other Aborigines as they climb over the burnt-out car of the children's father: two different games, two different cultures and a reminder of the event that has precipitated the children's plight. Roeg freezes frame three times in the film – the Aborigine's killing of the Kangaroo, the men's ogling of the woman at the weather station, the flight of birds after the shooting of the water buffalo for meat. Each time he invites us to make a mental connection between the three events: the Aborigine's state of nature; society's vulgar sexual attitudes; and the brutal impact of society on nature, and implicitly, on human nature, and 'natural' attitudes. Further annotation of these images and ideas is provided when Roeg cuts between the Aborigine's killing of an animal for food and a butcher's chopping meat; and between the men's craning for a sight of the woman's breasts at the weather station and the girl's naked bathing in a stream. The natural and the social are juxtaposed here, instinct versus inculcation; and what is also implied is both a description and comment on the process of human and social evolution. Like Stanley Kubrick's famous match-cut between the bone and the spaceship in *2001: A Space Odyssey*, it invites us to consider how we have arrived from there to here – from primitivism to civilization – and at what cost.

This particular theme is adumbrated in the film's marvellous opening. Nothing could be more conventional in outline: the father (John Meillon) at work, in his office; the mother at home, in the kitchen; girl and boy at school. Yet this opening is curiously full of tension, through its fragmented disclosure of visual information, its discordant and disorientating soundtrack (bits of Stockhausen's *Hymnen*, snippets from the radio that range from recipes to evolution, both themes that in an indirect way are to occur later). The main characters are introduced obliquely and, with hindsight, significantly, because the way they are introduced suggests a bit about their lives and how they will develop. The father's silence with his wife, his distractedness, his seeming indifference to his family betoken an inner mental pressure soon to explode. The girl's breathing exercises at school suggests a form of regimentation and control that will collapse when she finds herself stranded in the desert. The boy walks towards a huge tree: at a later stage in the film, the boy's sight of a tree will save the children's lives; still later a tree will be the focus for their games, as they become more acclimatized to their surroundings; still later, it will be the setting for the Aborigine's death.

One particular shot pans edgily past a wall to reveal the desert beyond. It is a shot with many dimensions and implications: a metaphoric suggestion of the inner desolation of modern man, up against a brick wall; the desert beyond the wall suggesting the repressed, hidden desolation of city life, or perhaps the savage lurking inside civilized man. It reminds me strongly of a passage, in D.H. Lawrence's magnificent study of Thomas Hardy (it is worth noting that Roeg as cameraman captured the look of Hardy better than anyone in the film of *Far from the Madding Crowd*):

> Upon the vast, incomprehensible pattern of some primal morality greater than ever the human mind can grasp is drawn the little, pathetic pattern of man's moral life and struggle, pathetic, almost ridiculous. The little fold of law and order, the little *walled city* [my italics] within which man has to defend himself against the waste enormity of nature, becomes always too small, and the pioneers venturing out with the code of the walled city upon them, die in the bonds of that code, free and yet unfree, preaching the walled city and looking to the waste.[8]

It is a description that is wonderfully applicable to the opening of *Walkabout*. The father's glimpse beyond the 'walled city' leads to his death, perishing in the 'waste enormity of nature', the desert, 'free and yet unfree, preaching the walled city' (in his madness the father affects the clipped business tones of his city life) but 'looking to the waste'. The girl/pioneer ventures out into the desert but she carries the values of the 'walled city' (a form of repression) and these will eventually get the upper hand and return her to the city. Even so, at the end, imprisoned by these values, she will still be 'looking to the waste', implicitly unsatisfied by her life, tormented and even traumatized by her sense of the potential and possibilities of an alternative life, but choosing instead to come to terms (as we all must) with the protection yet discontents of civilization.[9]

Following this opening, the father drives his children out to the desert and attempts to kill them before turning the gun on himself. It is a very tense, disturbing scene.

Small, inconsequential details build up a disturbing sense of threat and that something is wrong (it is a scene, incidentally, that is not in the novel, where the children are American and are stranded in the desert because their plane has crashed). The father keeps stopping the car ('You've stopped again . . . '); he seems uncomfortably aware of his daughter's sexuality (he looks suggestively at her legs); and he wordlessly snaps off the music on the car radio which the girl has switched on (we never see him talk in a friendly or intimate way with his children). The boy begins to play with his gun away from the car as the girl lays the cloth for the picnic. 'Bang! bang!' goes the boy, and then suddenly, as if from nowhere, real bullets are firing round him and, as will happen in *Don't Look Now*, a child's game ends in death. The violence seems to come out of nowhere, an eruption of the savage in man caused possibly by repression. As the children hide, the father's voice is heard, and the clipped tone and jagged rhythm (Meillon's vocal performance is superb here) is almost as disturbing as the shots themselves, suggestive of an inner violence, of a mind at the end of its tether ('Getting late . . . I've got to go now . . . You can't waste time . . . *We* have got to go now . . . I have got to go now'). A shot rings out: and although the children do not see it, they rightly assume their father has shot himself.

Characters in Roeg do literally go through mind-blowing experiences, lose their heads: it has happened in *Performance*, it happens here, and it will happen in its most extreme form in *Eureka*. The fate of the father also reflects the feeling in some of Roeg's films that people are *essentially* inexplicable, *fundamentally* unknowable. In *Walkabout*, this is consistent with the way the story is told from the children's point of view, and adds a dimension of terror and enigma to their experience. Roeg has also said that this feeling was a major impulse behind his attraction to the material of the later film *Insignificance*. 'My God', as he put it, describing his experience of watching the play on which the film was based, 'nobody knows a damn thing about anyone.'

The children must now proceed on their own through a desert which they will find is crackling with life, with creatures that comfort and others that threaten. A magical dissolve at one stage seems to soften a rock into a pillow for the sleeping boy. At another stage, a snake twines round a tree above the sleeping girl, as if anticipating the threat to her innocence. One thinks of D.H. Lawrence again: his poem 'Snake', in which a snake comes out of a dark hole, in one critic's words, 'to symbolise all that civilized society disowns, rejects'[10] and which is driven back into the darkness by the voice of education; and yet in Lawrence's eyes, is a lord of life, beautiful, pure, a force of energy. Like the Lawrence poem, *Walkabout* also concerns our repressed animal natures, our sensuality; and the contest between our natural selves and the 'pettiness' (Lawrence's word) that 'civilized' behaviour imposes on us. Roeg's visual reminder of civilization in the desert is the children's school uniform, which is also a reminder of the civilization they must unlearn if they wish to survive. 'We don't want people to think we're a couple of tramps,' says the girl, insisting on keeping up a smart appearance. But the boy replies, pertinently: 'What people?' The contrast between the girl and boy at this stage is a contrast between the girl's prim propriety and civilized restraint against the boy's more primitive, instinctive directness. 'We're lost, aren't we?' he says, to which she replies, untruthfully but keeping a stiff upper lip: 'No, of course not.' This contrast will be important when they first meet the Aborigine, but at the time we note the incongruity of civilized behaviour in an alien, 'uncivilized' landscape.

Exhausted and carried on his sister's back, the boy spies a water hole by a quondong tree. This inverted shot anticipates the way their perceptions are shortly to be turned upside down by their encounter with the Aborigine. The water saves them but it dries up overnight, and it is in the midst of their despair that the boy glimpses a shape in the distance. Figure, or mirage? 'Dad . . . ' whispers the boy: a lizard turns to look. The shot of the figure in the distance might be Roeg's homage to, or recollection of, his work on David Lean's desert movie, *Lawrence of Arabia*, and that famous first shot of Omar Sharif as a mysterious sliver of shadow emerging out of the sun-baked desert. (Later the boy will have a vision, or mirage, of some camels.) The dialogue too – about water, and Englishmen – has echoes of the Peter O'Toole-Omar Sharif exchange in *Lawrence*: this is Roeg's desert movie. 'We're English – English . . . can't you understand? Anyone can understand that,' says the girl to the Aborigine. 'Where is Adelaide?' Understandably, the Aborigine is nonplussed at the girl's over-sophisticated, over-civilized attempt at communication, and even the boy is exasperated by her priorities, her adult inclination to think ahead rather than attend to the immediate concern: 'Ask him for water!' In fact, the boy's more instinctive form of communication through gesture is much more effective. He mimes the action of drinking, and the Aborigine understands instantly. It is the beginning of their association, friendship and adventure.

Whereas our first sight in the film of the Aborigine is prolonged and enigmatic, his first appearance in the novel is more abrupt – he suddenly emerges about four feet away from them. The differences between film and novel generally are interesting and revealing about Roeg's overall interpretation.[11] In the novel, the children, Mary and Peter, are American and, as mentioned before, stranded in the desert because of a plane crash. In the film, they are given no names; they are English rather than American (or Australian); and they are stranded because of the suicidal madness of their father. These are significant differences. By giving them no names, Roeg makes them less individualized, more archetypal figures; in making them English, Roeg seems to emphasize the theme of sexual repression and trauma (which are traditionally seen as typically English problems – it is a film with much in common with Alexander Mackendrick's 1965 version of *A High Wind in Jamaica* and Joseph Losey's great 1970 film of *The Go-Between*[12]). He also emphasizes the contrast between their civilized demeanour and the surrounding wilderness; and in changing the fate of the father, Roeg seems to be looking ahead to a later mysterious suicide, which will resonate at the close of the film just as the father's death has exploded at the beginning. The novel, like the film, becomes on one level almost a documentary of bird, animal and plant life in the Australian desert which, the novelist Marshall says, 'was something very different from the desert of popular imagination' (the freshness of Roeg's camera-eye rises to the challenge of Marshall's imaginatively descriptive prose). However, unlike the novel, the film cross-cuts the desert experience with a social context – for example, the weather station – and this again emphasises the contrast between civilization and wilderness. It also satirizes civilization's trivial pursuits by contrasting them with the children's struggle for survival, a struggle that is simultaneously expanding their mental frontiers.

In the novel, the Aborigine's first impression of his white friends is that they are 'perhaps the last survivors of some peculiarly backward tribe'. It is similar to the alien's view of our world in *The Man Who Fell to Earth*. Like *Performance*, *Walkabout* deals with a clash of cultures, but a clash that almost becomes contact. Like most of Roeg's films, it is a weird love story in which communication is almost, but not quite, made. The Aborigine reacts to the girl's touch; she is aware of his nakedness; but his strange courtship dance before her, which has a sinuous sensuality quite distinct from the dead sexuality seen elsewhere (the wordless husband and wife at the beginning, the meteorologist at the weather station, the prostitute at the tourist market who tries to lure the Aborigine) frightens rather than liberates her. Now having reached a ghost town that has whispers of civilization, she has become less spontaneous, and she spurns the Aborigine's love with a request for 'water', and he echoes the word sadly in English. Water has no life-giving properties in this context: it is domestic rather than regenerative and requested in the tone of a colonialist exacting services from a perceived 'inferior'.

In the novel when the three first meet, there is the following passage:

> Brother and sister were products of the highest strata of humanity's evolution. In them the primitive had long ago been swept aside, been submerged by mechanization, been swamped by scientific development, been nullified by the standardized pattern of the white man's way of life. They had climbed a long way up the ladder of progress; they had climbed so far, in fact, that they had forgotten how their climb had started.[13]

In the film this image of the ladder is picked up in a strange story the boy tells. A boy climbs a ladder to try and hear what his mother is saying (he thinks she is blind and dumb but that she talks when he is out of the house); he still cannot hear her from outside the window; inadvertently he knocks over the ladder, and slips off the windowsill and breaks his neck. Roeg edits the story in a striking way, pretending the frame of the film is the page of a book so that, as the boy is talking, it is as if we are reading a moving picture book. Whereas in the novel, the ladder signifies the ladder of evolution away from our primitive forbears, in the film it is more a ladder of connection, in which communication and understanding are reached for but tragically give way beneath our feet. The Aborigine is to break his neck; the girl, like the mother in the story, is to stay cocooned within her own world, barricaded in her own civilization, her own inner blindness. Roeg does not insist on the parallelism – it is more a *divertissement* on the perils of communication, or even curiosity. But under the childlike veneer of the story is a disturbing adult allegory, just as the film offers a mature commentary on the discontents of civilization under the guise of a children's adventure.

The Aborigine has discovered the road and realizes that civilization is close, a realization which is reinforced when he witnesses the hunting and killing with long-range rifles of some animals. The death throes of the animals seem to foreshadow his knowledge of his own fate. (In the novel, it is the girl's terror of him that disables him 'for it could mean only one thing: that she had seen in his eyes an image: the image of the Spirit of Death.' In the film it seems more a general identification with the natural world and a feeling that so-called civilization renders him lifeless, an anachronism.) He dons what, to western eyes, looks like war paint and lies in a valley of bones, amongst the skeletons of dead animals. He appears before the girl, who is undressed and terrified and goes into a dance that seems to start out as courtship ritual (a plea for integration, for her to join him) but becomes, because of her reaction in the darkened hut, a dance of death. He dances to exhaustion, the war paint now a mask of tragedy. Finally, he will hang himself on a tree, thus completing the film's tree imagery of life and death, and recalling the mysterious suicide with which the film began. His suicide also takes the children by surprise. It happens in a kind of no-man's-land between city and desert, for each character feels he or she has nowhere to go. The link is emphasized by the fact that after the Aborigine's death, the children can for the first time talk about their father's death. 'Did he shoot himself? . . . Why did he?' asks the boy. 'I suppose he thought he was doing the best thing,' she replies.

Civilization now beckons and its first words are: 'Put that down . . . this is all private property . . . don't touch anything.' The children have returned to the world of ownership, possession and paranoia. There follows a brief scene of the children playing in an abandoned mine, a sort of brief transcendence of natural instinct amongst a graveyard of industrialization, until we are abruptly returned to the city. We suddenly realize that several years have passed and that the opening of the film is being reprised: life as vicious circle. The girl, now a grown woman, is in the kitchen, cutting meat, like her mother in the opening of the film. She is smoking, and wearing make-up, the war paint of civilization. Her husband comes in, talking excitedly about promotion – he seems to be what the 80s would call a 'yuppie' – but, as he speaks, the words fade, she looks away, and Roeg dissolves to an idealized memory: of herself, her brother, and the Aborigine, naked and unashamed, bathing in complete harmony, with their oppressive coating of civilization (their school uniforms) standing on sticks like scarecrows. Over the soundtrack we hear the words of part of a poem from A.E. Housman's *A Shropshire Lad*:

> That is the land of lost content,
> I see it shining plain,
> The happy highways where I went,
> And cannot come again.

The critic Roy Armes has commented on this finale: 'The ending is strikingly bleak: no communication is achieved and years later the desert is only a romanticized memory or dream for the girl who has followed her parents' life pattern.'[14] Perhaps 'bleak' is a little strong but at least it is a useful corrective against 'sentimental'. The sadness, as John Izod observes, is less for the loss of a perfect past than for the loss of a possible future.[15]

Walkabout has often been seen as a harbinger of one of the most interesting film phenomena of the 1970s – the resurgence of Australian film. Certainly in its complex response to landscape, which is both threatening and beautiful, and its sympathetic attitude to the Aborigine, it anticipates a number of trends of the Australian New Wave. It particularly anticipates many of the characteristics of Peter Weir's *Picnic at Hanging Rock*: (1975) the repressive, regimented school setting, the tense picnic, the fascination with bourgeoning sexuality, the enigmatic disappearances and deaths. In an interview in *Films Illustrated*, Peter Weir commented on certain similarities between his films and Roeg's: 'I reckon I could have made every one of his films and he could have made every one of mine.'[16] One can certainly see the connection in *Hanging Rock* and in Weir's *The Last Wave* (1977), where the use of the Aborigine as symbol of alien culture recalls *Walkabout*, where the hero with potential second sight evokes *Don't Look Now*, and where the strangely interpolated trial scenes look back to *Performance*. Even a later film such as Weir's

Hollywood debut *Witness* (1985) has a Roegish element to it: culture clash, contrasting visions, impossible love.

Ultimately, *Walkabout* seems a quintessential Roeg film, photographed with a fresh, instinctive childlike sense of wonder. It fits the classic narrative pattern of Roeg films with a main character of limited vision (in this case, the girl) being given a glimpse into a larger world than she has previously experienced – intimidating and dangerous, primitive more than civilized, uninhibited more than repressed, offering the possibility of liberty and psychic extension against the danger of chaos and madness. Roeg is sensitive to the criticism that he was equating the black boy with Rousseau's noble savage and saying that his life was better ('This would be too elementary') but he was, he says, exploring the different values of the white children and the black boy, and exploring the implications of a simpler form of life.

Implicitly, the movie is about the quality of modern life: its comforts, that we would miss if separated from them, as well as its pressures, that can lead to alienation and breakdown; its potential energy, conveyed by the bustle of city life, as well as its often overpowering devitalization, as if the city crushes the life out of its inhabitants. The theme is brought into sharp relief precisely through the city's contrast with the inquisitive, instinctive world of childhood and with a stark uncluttered landscape bristling with vitality and danger. Roeg's sympathies here would link him with two other great writers about childhood whom his films often either quote or allude to – William Blake and D.H. Lawrence – and the call of the natural uncivilized landscape will be evident again in *Castaway*. Like *A High Wind in Jamaica*, *Walkabout* is about a physical and psychological journey *ostensibly* towards, but *actually* away from, English values: a search for civilization that discovers, then must discard, something more liberating.

Don't Look Now (1973)

Nothing is what is seems . . . Seeing is believing . . . It's okay, I found the real world.
(John Baxter in *Don't Look Now*)

It's incredible you can't change your course.
(Laura Baxter)

What . . . is it . . . you fear?
(The Inspector in *Don't Look Now*)

I imagined him [John Baxter] *as somebody who might have been a Rhodes scholar and had perhaps met* [Laura's] *brother at Oxford, so their families had been linked that way. I wanted to have them be almost golden people, so that it became rather like the incident at Chappaquiddick. Like the Kennedy family. They were unprepared in life. Most people are, aren't they?*
(Nicolas Roeg)[1]

Julie Christie, Hilary Mason, Clelia Matania

The opening sequence of *Don't Look Now*, in which a young girl drowns in a pond at the end of her garden despite the frantic efforts of her father to save her, will be remembered by all who have seen it. It is as compelling an opening scene as that of David Lean's *Great Expectations* (1946), in which the convict springs from nowhere to grab the little boy in the graveyard, and it is as important for much the same reason. A lot of what will happen in the remainder of the film will

41

depend on the impact of this opening and the chill instilled by it, so that, when Roeg cuts back to it later, the original feelings of apprehension and suspense will immediately re-surface. Also, much of the film will develop clues and motifs established in that opening: the theme of drowning; the mystery of a red-clad figure on a transparency John Baxter (Donald Sutherland) is examining shortly before the accident, and which seems to rhyme with the image of his daughter in her red mac[2]; the intimations of second sight in Baxter, which give the audience a foretaste of later disaster, a premonitory vision of disturbing correspondences between disparate actions, and even objects and shapes, whose significance the main characters fail to see until too late.

This opening sequence does not appear in Daphne du Maurier's original short story, which begins with the husband and wife together in a café in Venice and becoming aware that a couple of old ladies are staring at them in a rather peculiar way. In the story the child dies of meningitis and not by drowning, as in the film. These alterations by the film's excellent scriptwriters, Allan Scott and Chris Bryant, make the child's death more dramatic and visual; more significantly, the death in the film seems in some way more the husband's fault.

In the story, Baxter's profession is not specified (he and his wife Laura are simply on holiday), whereas in the film, his work as a church restorer gathers cumulative resonance as the narrative develops. Also, whereas in the story the possibility of Baxter's having psychic powers is not mentioned until a third of the way through, in the film his second sight is strongly implied almost from the beginning: a strange look off the edge of the frame as if he is watching the images we are watching; a sharp reaction from him when, outside, his son rides over some glass; and then his movement to the door, as if sensing something is wrong, even before he knows for certain that his daughter is in danger. It is a second sight of which he is unaware or which he represses – he is perhaps a little too confident and self-assured in his circumscribed world. His wife Laura (Julie Christie) is more curious, more open to experience; even in this first scene, she is trying to find the answer to a question her daughter Christine has posed – 'If the world is round, why is a frozen pond flat?' In a brief shot, we see that Baxter is the author of a book called *Beyond the Fragile Geometry of Space*: his own sense of space and time in the film will come to seem increasingly fragile and he, like most Roeg protagonists, will be invited to go beyond it into a new sphere of perception.

The opening was originally written as a pre-credit sequence but rejected as such by Roeg, partly because he dislikes pre-credit scenes but mainly because he was insistent on retaining the specific sound-cut that bridges the sudden jump in the narrative both in time (some months have passed) and space (from England to Venice) – that is, the cut from Julie Christie's short scream on seeing her daughter, taking in the tragedy *instantly*, to the drill her husband is using in his work on the church in Venice. It is a cut that fires the viewer like a bullet into the future: future *shock* will be one of the film's main themes. Yet the two shots over the film's brief opening credits also warrant some attention. The first shot is a doom-laden forward zoom towards the pond, as the morning rain comes down. The second is inexplicable until later when we recognize the image as the window-shades of the Baxters' hotel room in Venice, with the evening sun glinting through them.

In retrospect, these two shots will serve as an indicator of the way the film plays with present and future time. Within five minutes, it becomes clear why the first shot has zoomed so menacingly towards that pond, as if sucked ineluctably towards it (a forewarning of the way Baxter himself will seem unable to change his course, will run head-first towards his doom?) But the second shot remains mysterious until a good forty minutes into the film. The first shot precedes the drowning; the second precedes the love scene: from premature death to the possibility of new birth, perhaps. Nevertheless, the most immediately striking thing is that the mystery of the opening shot is almost immediately explained, whereas the explanation for the mystery of the second shot is considerably delayed.

The significance of this is that it anticipates the way in which the film will show the present and the future operating side by side – what Robert Kolker has called a 'twice-told tale in which two perceptions of events – from within the film and from the outside – conflict and deform one another.'[3] One character will claim she can see into the future; another will reject such a gift as so much 'mumbo-jumbo', but may be psychic without being aware of it (in which case, at what point do his 'present' visions become his 'future' visions?) And we as audience, because of editing which forges a link between unlikely material and forces these uncanny correspondences on our attention, are endowed with second sight and our scepticism about extrasensory perception is broken down by filmic means.

At certain points in the film, it is not clear where we are in time: a flashback might actually be a flash-forward. For example, during the scene in which Laura meets for the first time the blind psychic sister Heather (Hilary Mason), Roeg cuts in a shot of a serious-looking Laura departing in a limousine. Is the shot a flashback – Laura leaving for the funeral of her daughter perhaps? (In its context, it seems so.) But might it not also be a flash-forward, a shot of her leaving for the funeral of her husband? It is, after all, the blind sister who is to warn that Baxter is in danger if he stays in Venice.

The marvellous love scene, in which the lovemaking is intercut with shots of the Baxters getting dressed and ready to go to dinner, is similarly ambiguous. Are the shots of dressing genuinely flash-forwards, or evidence of Baxter's pyschic gifts, simultaneously sensing the pleasure of the act and the anxiety of the aftermath? For although Laura glows in post-coital contentment (as both story and film make clear, it is the first time since the tragedy that husband and wife have felt able to make love), Baxter seems a little subdued and withdrawn, as if even then sensing that their pleasures are at an end and only danger awaits. Everything will build towards the turning point in the film, when John will see an image from the future (Laura and the two sisters *in mourning*) and fatally mistake it for an image from the present.

A few further points about those opening two shots. A setting shortly to be associated with death is followed by a shot of a setting later to be associated with marital love and possible rebirth: taken together, they represent the polarity between ominousness and salvation, apprehension and transcendence through which the film moves. They also represent the identifiable alongside the inexplicable, the ordinary alongside the slightly bizarre. There is a moody anticipation here of the characterization of the two strange sisters the Baxters are to meet in Venice, the one practical and down to earth (Clelia Matania), the other strange and unnerving (Hilary Mason). This might be extended to include a consideration of the way the sisters are presented in the film, where at times they seem eccentric and harmless, and at other times possibly malevolent and menacing. The blind sister, Heather, comments on the two possible attitudes to her psychic powers: they are a gift but they can also be a curse. This duality is further extended into the reactions of Laura and John Baxter to the sisters and particularly to Heather's paranormal claims. For Laura, the sisters are helpful, wise, genuine, and Heather's psychic reassurances about her dead daughter give Laura a peace for which she has been searching. For John, on the other hand, the sisters are threatening and grotesque. At one stage, he is struggling with a gargoyle on the church exterior when he spies them out of the corner of his eye, and the instant association speaks volumes about Baxter's attitude. At another stage, he spots them in a church and covers up his eyes so as not to see them: coming upon him, Laura thinks he is praying and says jokingly, 'You hypocrite . . . ' There is a lot in that moment: Baxter's attempting to wish away the evidence of his own eyes by affecting a *wilful* blindness; Laura's mistaken perception of what he is actually doing; the church ambience, which picks up the theme of faith that is to be developed in a wider sense in the film.

Finally, the two opening shots pick up two motifs that will be important in the film: water and windows. There is a hymn that goes:

'A man that looks on glass
On it may stay his eye
Or if he wishes through it pass
And then the heavens espy'.

The lines are directly applicable to John Baxter – the limits of his vision, the potential of his perceptions, if he can let himself go. Also applicable is a comment made by Roeg about the motif of broken glass in the film: 'That particular thing was absolutely conscious. It stemmed from a story, a personal story. A friend of mine might have been able to save . . . to prevent a dreadful incident . . . he said . . . *if* he'd been able to break some glass at the time. Apart from any symbolic quality, glass sets up a sensation of fear, of something dangerous and brittle. This is built into everyone. Almost everyone has a fear of shattered glass. Mirrors and glass, glass especially, so fragile . . . so firm at one moment and so dangerous the next.'[4]

In a review of *Don't Look Now* in *Films and Filming*, Gordon Gow commented that he thought Roeg's cross-cutting in the love scene 'might stand as a classic study piece'.[5] This is no less true of the opening scene, which illustrates practically every facet of montage as an expressive device in the cinema. The situation is that of a typical Sunday afternoon, in which husband and wife occupy themselves indoors after lunch (he is inspecting some slides; she is consulting a book) whilst the children play at the end of the garden outside. The two actions take place simultaneously but as the film cross-cuts between them, Roeg is careful to show the *spatial* relationship (the fragile geometry of space?) between the two actions – in other words where these settings are in relation to each other. This will be crucial when the viewer realizes how far the pond is from the house and the ground Baxter has to cover to try to save his daughter. The action is represented sequentially but is also fragmented when the film momentarily concentrates on a particular detail: for example, the transparency Baxter is inspecting, with its small red figure seated in a church, that seems to be impinging ominously on his, and our, attention. The linking of shots is mainly chronological, but sometimes shots are linked by association: for example, the girl tosses a ball outside, whilst inside the father tosses some cigarettes; the mother makes a gesture with her fingers over her mouth, and the daughter outside makes a similar gesture; the son bends over his bike, and the father bends over his transparency. Shots are also linked by similarity or contrast of shape and physical appearance, the main example here being the linking of the girl Christine in her red mac and the red-hooded figure in the slide. There is further symmetry in the arrangement of the two parents together inside the house and the girl and boy outside: a contrast between large and small, reinforced by Christine's playing with her doll's house, with the real house visible in the distance.

The montage also creates a particular rhythm. The opening shots of children playing are quite leisurely, and this tempo is reinforced by Pino Donaggio's simple, hesitant main theme, sounding like a child picking out a tune on the piano. The shots seem to link smoothly at the beginning but, by the middle of the scene, shots are more fragmented, nervous and seem to collide more than cohere. This manipulation of tempo will be felt most agonizingly in Roeg's use of slow motion, when the father has been too slow to rescue his daughter and his grief seems excruciatingly prolonged; and also the calculated delay in giving the mother's reaction, with a number of cut-backs to her that increase the sense of anxiety and the impact when she does learn. When she sees, she sees *instantly*: it is an important contrast to her husband, who senses in advance, but reacts slowly to his intuitions and finally sees too late.

The effectiveness of the scene is primarily conveyed through Roeg's mastery of montage. By establishing connections between two apparently unconnected places of action, the montage generates atmosphere and suspense. Two seemingly realistic events become weird and uncomfortable because the montage insists on their unaccountable similarities; the stories are somehow connected but the characters are separated; we in the audience see visual correspondences, which are clearly significant, but the characters do not. Through these connections and Baxter's subdued reactions of strange apprehension, as if he is inwardly hearing or seeing something but does not act, the editing creates a powerful sense of anxiety. The anxiety is reinforced by repetition, particularly of the shot of the transparency accompanied by Donnagio's ghostly thematic motif. At one moment we are shown an inverted reflection of the girl Christine as she runs alongside the pond, and it is a chilling shot on two levels: a premonition/anticipation of her falling into the water; and an inverted image that links her even more strongly to the transparency (for, of course, transparencies are inserted upside down, to be flipped over by the projector). The boy rides over the glass; the husband knocks over his drink onto the transparency; the girl slips into the pond. Broken glass/spilt drink/ drowning: a progression of terrifying logic. When the drink spills onto the transparency the colour on the transparency begins to spread: it seems like blood. The transparency seems to acquire a malign quality – it is shown thirteen times. And the 'normality' of a casual Sunday afternoon – signified by the shot of the piled-up dinner-plates – has been completely subverted.

The opening is of crucial importance to the whole film. The sense of pain established in the opening will carry through to the end, making it difficult to imagine that anything but tragedy could await after such a scene. At various later stages, the film will quote from that scene, and amplify some of its imagery: for example, the couple's seeing a dead body being pulled up out of a Venetian canal, which inevitably recalls Christine's lifeless body being pulled too late out of the water. The link between Christine and the red-hooded figure is first established here, and it is a link that will lead John Baxter to his death. When the drink drops onto the transparency and the colour begins to run, it spreads into a particular shape – the shape of Venice, as seen later on the map on the Inspector's wall when he talks to Baxter. Has Baxter foreseen his *own* death, as well as his daughter's? There is a curious similarity in the ways the opening and closing scenes develop: in the beginning is the end. As in this opening scene, the son and wife will be outside the main action, the son injured, the wife behind a barrier, whilst John Baxter will rush to the aid of a red-clad figure, only to encounter death. At the end, Baxter, on the point of death, will glimpse an array of images from the main body of the narrative. They not only signify the memory flashes of a dying man as his life passes before his eyes, but they also signify the moment of understanding: what all these disparate images meant and portended, how they all fitted. The mosaic of meaning – which could serve as a definition of montage – finally comes together in Baxter's head.

The main action takes place in Venice. The city has never been more dramatically or expressively used on film. 'One of the things I love about Venice', says the blind sister Heather when Baxter is taking her back to her hotel (the speech is not in du Maurier's story), 'is that it's so safe for me to walk. The sounds . . . My sister hates it. She says it's like a city in aspic after a dinner party, and all the guests are dead and gone. It frightens her . . . Milton loved this city, did you know that?' The description of Venice as a 'city in aspic' is an evocation worthy of Edgar Allan Poe: indeed, Heather's description conjures up images from the finale of Roger Corman's Poe adaptation that Roeg photographed, *The Masque of the Red Death* – diners in paralysis after a banquet, at the mercy of a killer in a red mask. It is 'safe' for Heather to walk in Venice – that is, safe for the physically blind but not, as will shortly be shockingly demonstrated, for the psychically blind.

Roeg's treatment of Venice in his movie might be set alongside and contrasted with that of three artists whose work seems to invite inevitable comparison with that of Roeg's: David Lean, Joseph Losey and D.H. Lawrence. In David Lean's *Summer Madness* (1955), Venice is the city of the travel brochure, of summery romance, whereas in Roeg's film it is a Venice out of season, with a hotel manager out of sorts who seems a forerunner of John Cleese's Basil Fawlty and indeed of Rowan Atkinson's hotel manager in *The Witches*. (Roeg suggested to the actor, Leopold Trieste, that he should be a hotel manager who does not like the guests.) In Joseph Losey's *Eve* (1962), Venice is a city of dark baroque decadence, whereas in Roeg, it is a city in peril, stagnant and submerging and in the process (like the hero) dragging up fearsome things from its hidden depths – rats, corpses. It is also a city *of* peril, in which the hero will lose himself in dark narrow streets and alleys, a city in which to die: it is Roeg's *Death in Venice*. For D.H. Lawrence, in his poem 'Pomegranates', Venice is the 'abhorrent, green slippery city'. More remarkably; he describes it in a letter as 'very lovely to look at, but very stagnant as regards life . . . Italy feels very unsure, and for the first time I feel a tiny bit frightened of what they might do, in a sudden, ugly, *red* [my italics] mood.'[6] It is one of those sudden, ugly, *red* moods that will kill Baxter. In other respects, *Don't Look Now* has a strange similarity to one of Lawrence's most enigmatic short stories, 'England, my England'. Both works have heroes who are estranged from their home environment and who foresee, without being able to avert, tragedies directed at their children; and the bold experimentation with narrative time in both (Lawrence makes wonderful use of an extended, concealed flashback) gives enormous force to their similarly hallucinatory finales in both of which the heroes, at the point of death, make an 'effort to catch at straws of memory, straws of life from the past'. Baxter's horrifying end certainly echoes Lawrence's: 'The world all blood, and the blood all writhing with death.'[7]

If the city of Venice is an important correlative for the mood and action of the movie, an equally important dimension is the religious sub-theme, an element quite absent from the original story. All of the main characters are connected to religion in some way. John Baxter is a restorer of church artworks. Laura lights candles for her daughter Christine and at one stage kisses the bishop's ring, which prompts him to ask the question: 'Are you a Christian, Laura?' The bishop (Massimo Serato) is a powerful, quietly charismatic character, stately but also sensual, and a man much more interested in the spirit than the artefacts of the church, unlike John Baxter. Also unlike Baxter, the bishop believes in prophecy – although he adds, 'I wish I didn't have to'. The prophetic sister Heather is deeply religious, and her second sight ('a gift from the good Lord') is linked to her faith: she senses the presence of some power beyond herself. In this sense, the film is about faith, the willingness to surrender rationalism and be open to new avenues of awareness. But for John Baxter, *seeing is believing*': a 'belief' that will literally be his undoing, since the turning point of the film will be his seeing something – Laura and the two sisters – whose significance he does not penetrate until too late.

The importance of the religious sub-theme is not simply to emphasize the theme of faith but to furnish an ironic context in which the limits of the hero's vision can be perceived. He might restore a church's mosaics – the film is a mosaic – but his interest is more aesthetic than spiritual, unlike the bishop who just watches politely until he is nearly brained by a piece of falling scaffolding. Indeed, Baxter's restoration of the church might be seen as analogous to his attempt to restore his married life to some semblance of order, but religion, faith, prophecy give no meaning to his life. Accordingly the film's religious aspect emphasizes, by contrast, the meaninglessness of Baxter's death. It is the most absurd death imaginable, a death with the bizarre but inevitable illogic of the question that opened the picture: 'If the world is round, why is a frozen pond flat?'

This ending has often been criticized as being inherently preposterous ('One cannot go through life worrying about being killed by a grotesque dwarf,' comment Marshe Kinder and Beverle Houston sternly in their review of the film).[8] Yet for Roeg the very ludicrousness of the death was the thing that won him over to the story, because he likes the absurd and wanted to clap when he read the story's last line: 'The hammering and the voices and the barking dog grew fainter and "Oh God", he thought, "what a bloody silly way to die . . . '" It is still a scene that can chill, as an expected child turns to reveal an old, old face.

The dwarf is one of a number of such aliens in Roeg's films, who are part of but do not belong in the real world – Newton in *The Man Who Fell to Earth*, the witches in *The Witches*, and, as a benevolent version, the Aborigine in *Walkabout*. The dwarf seems also a Fellini-esque grotesque, and a Rumpelstiltskin whom the Alien describes so fascinatingly in the novel of *The Man Who Fell to Earth*: 'that evil little dwarf who came from nowhere . . . to save the princess's life with his unheard-of knowledge, the stranger whose final purpose was to steal the princess's child . . . '⁹

The disquieting combination of Christianity and absurdity in the movie is also reminiscent of Shakespeare's *King Lear*, another work in which the death of a beloved daughter breaks a father's heart, and which, more fundamentally, is about sight and blindness – about people who stumble when they can see and others who become hyper-perceptive when blind. Like *Lear* too, it has bits of black comedy. *Lear* courts laughter during Gloucester's 'jump' from what he thinks is Dover Cliff but is actually level ground, and so does Roeg at moments such as that at the very end of the film when Heather is left to stumble momentarily on her own, only to be retrieved by an ever-fussy Wendy.

Don't Look Now is a tale of polarities and paradoxes. Baxter saves churches: the church (belief, faith, prophecy) cannot save him. He rescues buildings from death and decay whilst he himself seems to head straight for destruction, towards a self-willed death, like Turner in *Performance* and the Aborigine in *Walkabout*. After Baxter's narrow escape from a fall, he stands outside the church with the bishop, and another polarity proclaims itself: the sobriety of Catholicism and the slapstick of Chaplin. A Chaplin poster on the church wall sports the heading 'One Against All'. (Chaplin will be alluded to again in the later film *Eureka*.) Does this refer to Baxter, as the stoical secular man in an uncomprehending absurdist universe? Or does it allude to the dwarf, another 'little fellow' who will strike out at the world, even, like Monsieur Verdoux, to the point of murder?

On its first appearance, because of their almost simultaneous openings, *Don't Look Now* tended to be linked with the Gothic extravagance of *The Exorcist* (1973). In fact, it belongs directly in the tradition of some of the most stylish of British horror films. It evokes the 'I've been here before' feeling of *Dead of Night* (1945). It is as obsessed with images and looking as Michael Powell's *Peeping Tom*. It shares, with Jack Clayton's *the Innocents* (1961), the death of children and the theme of innocence, and also the violence and ferocious pessimism of Michael Reeve's *Witchfinder General* (1966). It also has a kinship with Peter Sasdy's *Hands of the Ripper* (1971), the most remarkable film to come out of Hammer Studios. Sasdy's film similarly has a sceptical, analytical hero whose rationalism will bring him to the brink of destruction; similarly it has a key character who is blind, and leading characters who are called John and Laura; and similarly it parades an array of religious symbols that gathers to a remarkable finale, in Sasdy's film at St Paul's, where the whispering gallery is used almost as evocatively as the sounds of Venice in *Don't Look Now*.

Horror has traditionally brought colour and blood to the cheeks of British film. Just as George Orwell thought it odd, and very English, that the most famous battle poem in the English language, 'The Charge of the Light Brigade', should be about an army that charges in the wrong direction, so it is equally odd, and English, that the most famous love story in the British cinema, David Lean's *Brief Encounter* (1945), is one in which nothing happens. Maybe *Don't Look Now* is Roeg's riposte to Lean. Is it accidental that Laura in *Don't Look Now* (whose name, incidentally, is the same as Lean's heroine) meets the two sisters in exactly the same way that Celia Johnson meets Trevor Howard in *Brief Encounter* – grit in the eye? (It is not that way in the du Maurier story.) And that what follows the meeting is not frustration but the most passionate love scene in British film? It would not be the first Roeg movie to allude to, but also subvert, the David Lean tradition. *Don't Look Now* shows he can tell a good yarn, not in the traditional style of humanist realism and classical restraint, but with a Gothic flamboyance and uninhibited sensuality.

The Man Who Fell To Earth (1976)

These films seemed more and more common lately; and like so many popular magazines, more and more wildly chauvinist – more committed than ever to the fantastic lie that America was a nation of God-fearing small towns, efficient cities, healthy farmers, kindly doctors, bemused housewives, philanthropists, millionaires.

'My God', he said aloud. 'My God, you frightened, self-pitying hedonists. Liars! Chauvinists! Fools!'
(Walter Tevis *The Man Who Fell to Earth*)[1]

In Breughel's Icarus, for instance . . . the expensive delicate ship that must have seen something amazing, a boy falling out of the sky, had somewhere to get to, and sailed calmly on.
(W.H. Auden, *Musée des Beaux Arts*)

At the end of the screening of The Man Who Fell to Earth, *Barry Diller* [head of production at Paramount] *turned to me reproachfully and said: 'You promised me a linear narrative.' It was the first time I had heard the phrase.*
(Michael Deely, British Lion Executive)[2]

The Man Who Fell to Earth was the first-ever British financed movie to be made in the United States. When **David Bowie** it appeared in Britain, the critical response was divided, ranging from guarded praise (*The Times*) and baffled enthusiasm (*The Sunday Times*) to outright dismissal (*The New Statesman*). The two main publications of the British Film Institute, *Sight and Sound* and *Monthly Film Bulletin* are usually of one accord when it comes to critical evaluation, but they completely parted company over this film. *Sight and Sound* suggested that 'not all the pieces fit, and the metaphysical games with love and time create more strangeness than the film can contain but a wealth of possibilities survive.'[3] On the other hand, Jonathan Rosenbaum in *Monthly Film Bulletin* thought it 'an extremely photogenic mess, full of sound and fury, signifying nothing.'[4]

Undoubtedly, part of the problem for critics and audience was simply unravelling the plot. The story is that of an alien from a dying planet who falls to earth in a bid to save his family and his people. He makes a fortune in order to construct a spacecraft that will enable his people to come to earth and save themselves from extinction. In the 1963 novel of Walter Tevis (perhaps best known as author of *The Hustler* and *The Color of Money*), the alien's purpose is also to save the world from destroying itself ('We are certain beyond all reasonable doubt that your world will be an atomic rubble heap in no more than thirty years if you are left to yourselves').[5] But in the film the purpose of the spacecraft is never made very clear. In his plot synopsis for the *Monthly Film Bulletin*, Rosenbaum tentatively suggests that 'Newton intimates that he came to Earth because his race was dying from a lack of water and that his space programme is designed to return him to his wife and child.' But that makes no sense at all. When the film was released in the States, audiences were provided with a sheet of 'explanations' to help them through the movie. One doubts very much if it helped.

The plot does not seem to have interested Roeg and his screenwriter Paul Mayersberg very much. Like *Walkabout*, it is another Blakeian film about the loss of innocence, the Fall. Like *Don't Look Now*, it has a hero of extra sensory, or hypersensitive, perception bound by the limits of terrestrial experience. It is another surreal story in a real setting, the kind of two-level narrative Roeg likes. Once again he confronts the 'normal' world with an alternative 'alien' one: it was pop culture in *Performance*, Aboriginal life in *Walkabout*, the psychic world in *Don't Look Now*. The difference in this case is the point of view. The story is seen mostly through the eyes of an alien, so that our familiar universe begins to look more and more unearthly and strange. Also, the brief flashbacks to life on the alien's planet have a tenderness and sentiment that is noticeably absent from the scenes of life on Earth. Obviously these are subjective, possibly idealized visions, but certainly the love scenes in *The Man Who Fell to Earth* have an obsessive ugliness and aggression that contrasts with the gentler atmosphere of the alien's planet. Indeed, 'love scenes' is a misnomer. *Don't Look Now* has a love scene, beautiful and fulfilling. *The Man Who Fell to Earth* has sex scenes, shallow, shrill and desperate.

Yet the alien (Davie Bowie), who is to call himself Thomas Jerome Newton, is perhaps not all that different from other Roeg protagonists, who are characteristically, in R.P. Kolker's words, 'aliens in a strange land, trying to make sense of their perceptions and failing'.[6] There might even be an unusual measure of identification between hero and director. In his book *National Heroes* (London 1984), Alexander Walker declared himself baffled by one particular detail, namely: 'Why, one wondered, did this heavenly body burden himself with an English accent on his visitation to America? It was typical of the Nicolas Roeg-Paul Mayersberg screenplay that it should provide a superabundance of peripheral data without addressing itself to this insistent illogicality.'[7] The simple answer to the question might be that the alien is given an English accent so as not to overtax David Bowie's acting ability. But what if Roeg also sees the alien as a surrogate of himself, an Englishman with a piercing eye in an overpowering and awesome American environment, who, as it were, loses sight of his goal, who, like Icarus[8] in Breughel's painting and Auden's poem (both of which are shown in the film in a book published by Newton's company World Enterprise Books), falls by the wayside? Certainly critics often talk of Roeg as if he were like Icarus, flying too high, overreaching himself, and plunging to the depths. Or to put it another way round, what if Roeg feels that we are all aliens, or in a sense alienated? The brother from another planet becomes then simply a metaphor for man's existential isolation.

The opening of the film suggests global vastness, as a creature is ejected from a spacecraft and hurtles through the fragile geometry of space. The alien lands in a huge lake and is barely noticed, like Icarus in Auden's poem. He has come from the stars to earth, whilst mankind is heading in the opposite direction, an early hint that extraterrestrial and earthlings are going to find it difficult to make contact within the same orbit. We next see him on the top of a hill, like a hero out of a Western. The film will continue shifting genre like this beneath our feet — from science fiction, to Western, to horror film, to conspiracy thriller — and the Western echoes will reappear when Newton is crossing America with his housekeeper Mary-Lou (Candy Clark) and has a vision of early settlers. At this early point, it establishes him as a time-traveller as well as a being of superior intelligence. It also suggests Newton as a lone figure in America caught in a time warp between pioneering nostalgia and future shock. Maybe *The Man Who Fell to Earth* can be read as the unflattering sci-fi contribution to the American Bicentennial, just as Robert Altman's *Buffalo Bill and the Indians* (1976) can be read as the unflattering, Western contribution. The modern pioneers would be the United States' scientists and its space-travellers, but these 'pioneers' are going nowhere in *The Man Who Fell to Earth*; an overheard comment on Newton's spacecraft later in the film is: 'Why the hell do they have to build these things . . . it's such a waste . . . such a waste of money.'

The film's slippery surface is emphasized when the alien has to slide down a gravelly slope towards a road. As he does so, the camera reveals that his landing has not been unobserved. He is being watched, by a mysterious unidentified man who will appear only once more in the film, at Newton's bedside towards the end. Perhaps nothing indicates Newton's otherworldly naivety more than his claim later when being interrogated by government officials that: 'I came alone . . . nobody saw me.' For in our modern technological age, in which communications make us all inhabitants of a global village, and in which political surveillance has in some parts of the world made privacy a thing of the past, nothing, it seems, goes unobserved. 'Nothing is true; everything is permitted,' said *Performance*. 'Nothing is secret; everyone is paranoid,' says *The Man Who Fell to Earth*.

There are two particular ways the film will develop the motif of watching and being watched. Newton obsessively watches a multitude of TV screens: it is the way he picks up his knowledge of Earth behaviour. There are a cluster of thematic resonances implied in the films he watches: *Billy Budd* (innocence throttled); *The Third Man* (friendship betrayed); *The Sound Barrier* (through difficulties to the stars – this is Roeg's typically inverted version of David Lean: through stars to difficulties); Billy Wilder's *Love in the Afternoon* ('I think people should always behave as if they were between planes,' says Gary Gooper's sexual philanderer – Newton is between planes, but his extraterrestrial sexual fidelity is a contrast to human promiscuity). TV images become his reality. But they overwhelm him with information, to the point where he will cry, 'Get out of my mind, all of you!' The more he sees, the less he seems to know. Indeed, the film seems to operate in the same way. It piles on imagery so lavishly that we are left dazed and confused by the concatenation of conflicting signals. Just as the alien finally cannot make sense of what is going on, nor can we. R.P. Kolker regards this as another of Roeg's 'twice-told tales', in the sense that, whereas we become steadily withdrawn from the film and finally outside it – barely able to follow, and completely unable to identify with, the narrative – Newton remains trapped within it, unable to escape in time as well as in space, for, in contrast with the characters around him, he seems not to age.

The second implication of the watching motif is simply its contribution to the film's gathering sense of paranoia. Newton has come up with nine inventions (among them, the self-developing film) and, with the expertise and help of his patents' lawyer Oliver Farnsworth (Buck Henry), has transformed the communications industry in America. This, however, has brought him to the attention of a mysterious Syndicate who see Newton's World Division Enterprises as a dangerous monopoly that could subvert the American economy. 'They have to take a wider view,' insists the Syndicate of Newton's too private enterprise, 'but remember this is not the Mafia. We're determining social ecology. This is modern America and we intend to keep it that way.' Yet their eventual strong-arm tactics are no different from those of the Mafia. (Remember that conversation in *The Godfather* when Al Pacino's Michael is explaining to Diane Keaton's Kay that his father, the Don, is no different from any other powerful man. 'Other powerful men don't have people killed,' says Kay, to which Michael replies, 'Now who's being naive'.) The oblique attack on corporate America in the film is the closest Roeg had come this far to an overt political statement, but perhaps this ties in more with the general theme of betrayal throughout the film. Newton is double-crossed by an enterprise culture that finds him too enterprising, and sold out by a science colleague, Bryce (Rip Torn), whom he trusts but who will take a secret photo of him and call in the authorities. It all gives another dimension to the wan flashbacks of his own planet, in which nostalgia for home alternates with visions of the betrayals of his new society.

When Newton lands on earth, he lands in what looks like a dying landscape: is the earth heading for destruction in the manner of his own planet? He passes what appear to be the remains of a carnival and is disconcerted by a drunk – who looks the more civilized here? – before falling asleep on a porch seat outside a local shop. When an old lady appears, to open up, he follows her into the shop. Time suddenly seems out of joint. The door is a bit mysterious to Newton. When the old lady pulls open a drawer, a gun is disclosed, a matter-of-fact, blunt emblem of the savage society he has entered. The jerky point-of-view camera movement as Newton moves through the shop projects us momentarily into his disorientation, confusion, fascination. The old lady who serves him immediately undercuts the notion of 'alien', for with her beads and a face crisscrossed with the lines of age, she actually looks stranger than he does. Maybe we are all, in some fundamental way, strange to each other and, for that matter, strangers, zooming to our private destinies, like Chas and Turner in *Performance*, the girl and the black boy in *Walkabout*: even the most intimate of love scenes in *Don't Look Now* is crosscut with the pair's post-coital separation and contemplation, coupling provocatively intercut with isolation. Moreover, the old lady in the shop cheats Newton, clearly paying him far less for the ring than it deserves. It is a harbinger of the subsequent betrayals to come.

The meeting later with Farnsworth is another strange encounter. The most striking feature of Farnsworth is his pebble glasses that enlarge his eyes disconcertingly as Newton approaches with his proposal: is this the deformation brought about by the greed within Farnsworth? As Farnsworth studies the ideas, Newton looks out at the American skyline and a segment of 'Venus: Bringer of Peace' from Holst's *The Planets Suite* is heard over the soundtrack (earlier we have briefly heard the ominous rhythms of 'Mars: Bringer of War': is the alien visitor friend or foe?) It is an ambiguous moment: does the music betoken Newton's, or the city's, strangeness? When he offers to replace Farnsworth's antiquated music system, but by deducting the cost from Farnsworth's salary, the lawyer comments drily: 'Perhaps you're not so different after all, Mr Newton.' It is an ironic line in context, but also an ominous one. Newton will actually be driven towards conformity, in a sort of *1984* cycle of betrayal, incarceration, brainwashing and experiment.

Farnsworth utters another ironic/ominous line shortly

afterwards when his association with the 'gift horse', Newton, is hitting its stride. 'When Mr Newton came into my apartment', he says, 'my life went straight out of the window.' That is how Farnsworth's life *will* go, when he is thrown out of his window by the mobsters. Like Newton, he will be another man who falls, heavily, to earth. Just before his death, the mobsters take off the emblem of Farnsworth's greed, his glasses – he will not be needing them anymore. 'Those are my eyes,' Farnsworth wails: Newton is similarly to be semi-blinded by the clumsy experimenting of the government officials. Perception and imperception are important themes in the film, particularly, as we have seen, when they are linked – when a veritable barrage of visual imagery serves only to short-circuit understanding.

Another key theme is transformation. If Farnsworth's life is overturned by Newton, a fate perhaps anticipated by the inverted close-up of Newton before he enters the shop of the old lady to begin his transactions, it will eventually be Newton's life that will be most thoroughly made over. Beginning as an alien of higher intelligence with laudable intentions and tender memories, at the end he will be that most archetypal of American successes (like Jeff Rink in *Giant*): the isolated alcoholic tycoon. Like David Lean's Lawrence, he has gone native.

Newton has gone native: the movie, alas, goes haywire. Whereas Lean is a humanist, Roeg is a modernist and perhaps that is where the problem of critical and public acceptance lies. Is there enough narrative momentum to sustain *The Man Who Fell to Earth* or, later, *Eureka* or *Track 29*? Are the structures too discursive, too idea-oriented rather than character-oriented? The sinister Syndicate begins to get apprehensive about Newton's Corporation because it is 'technologically overstimulated'. Might one say the same about Roeg's film?

Roeg's style here verges uncomfortably on self-parody. The intercutting during the sex scenes, unlike the intercutting of the love scene in *Don't Look Now*, seems more like *coitus interruptus*: not expansion, but an inability to concentrate on the matter in hand. (It is also vaguely misogynistic and anti-youth: Bryce's sexual attraction seems more middle-aged male wish-fulfilment than anything credibly dramatized.) When his energetic sexual bout with a student is cross-cut with Newton's uneasy watching of a Kabuki sword display, we do get the point: but somehow the harsh impersonality of the imagery, its blatant phallicism, seems overblown. A later sexual encounter between Newton and Mary-Lou is accompanied by guns being fired with blanks: explosive but empty, like the relationship now (unlike Chas in *Performance*, who is 'a bullet', Newton is now 'a blank'), but the brutal coldness of the imagery makes the couple seem even less appealing than they are. Then again, when Newton and Mary-Lou have a row, and Newton angrily knocks away a pan of cookies, the match-cut Roeg inserts between slow-motion floating cookies and floating aliens in space seems bizarre and incongruous rather than eloquent or moving. The connection is made between Newton's deteriorating behaviour on earth and the suffering and neglect on his planet, but the imagery trivializes rather than enlarges the connection.

The wayward style goes with the film's lack of narrative energy or forward propulsion. This has partly to do with the way Paul Mayersberg changed the character of Dr Bryce from what it was in the original novel. Mayersberg felt Bryce was little more than a plot device, to investigate Newton and to feed the alien questions as an aid to plot exposition, with the result that he had little character of his own. This is certainly a danger with that kind of role, but unfortunately he seems to have gone too far the other way. Now the emphasis is on friendship ('friendship is the most profound form of detection,' says Mayersberg[9]), and the detective element is so underplayed that the momentousness of the mystery evaporates. Unfortunately, Bryce is introduced more as a libido than as a character. Although he later suggests that 'my mind had developed a libido of its own' – in the film's increasing use of voice-over, as if to cover up some structural holes – the relationship between him and Newton barely registers, which makes the impact of Bryce's betrayal correspondingly weaker.

The relationship between Newton and Mary-Lou seems no more successful or interesting. It will be Mary-Lou who introduces him to gin and religion. Together they will sing 'Jerusalem' and about building a 'green and pleasant land', which is what Newton is trying to do. Yet the film is unduly harsh towards Mary-Lou. It poeticizes Newton's staring at the stars, but when Mary-Lou opines that, when she looks at the stars, it makes her think there is a God, acting and direction contrive to make the sentiment look trite. Moreover, whilst the other characters age more or less naturally and gracefully, the make-up job on the now bloated Mary-Lou seems grotesque and unduly unsympathetic.

If Newton is adrift from his family, it is curious that all the other main characters are separated from family too – they are displaced persons and, in a sense, floating as aimlessly through space as Newton himself. The only exception to this is the head of the Syndicate, Peters, whose family life we see, but this sidetracking on a minor character is more distracting than illuminating.

It is not that the scenes with Dr Bryce and Mary-Lou are irrelevant: one can make a case out for all of them as having some relation to the film's overall themes. It is more that they just do not fit together. Point and counterpoint, surface and inner meaning are not quite in balance. One can see a certain appropriateness, for example, in the use of the song 'Try to Remember' as Newton travels deeper into America: he must try to remember where he came from and the mission he has undertaken. But both the song (trite) and the image of the galloping white horse to connote freedom (cliché) make the overall effect seem excessively sentimental. Maybe it is Roeg's way of suggesting that Newton is becoming more Americanized, but irony requires a lighter touch.

Although the film is full of fine things and ideas (Newton as Gatsby, the reclusive hero living in a house across the lake, or Mary-Lou's accusation that Newton is an alien being accompanied by her throwing her *wig* at him), there seems something in the narrative trajectory of the project that defeats Roeg. He cannot help aping Newton's dilemma: he too becomes overwhelmed by the images in his head; confused by the world around him; trying unsuccessfully to take American industry (implicitly, the film industry? film narrative?) in a new direction and into a new dimension; but finally drifting helplessly into alienation. A man who fell from the sky with mind-blowing ideas is seen finally in an image that encircles his world within the rim of his fedora hat. The friends whose lives he has initially expanded and transformed are now parodies: Farnsworth splattered on a sidewalk, Mary-Lou puffed out and made up, and Bryce as a departmental store Father Christmas. A director who has started out with a blaze of brilliance has ended, seemingly, in an exhausted heap, having lost his narrative thread and gone through the motions of techniques that seem increasingly strained and arbitrary.

Bad Timing (1980)

The title of that film was originally different [Illusions] . . .
I woke up one day and thought of Bad Timing *which
sounds exactly like the right title — for my career. Now
there was a film I really thought was one to which there
would be a different response. Whilst filming I felt sure
that this was one for the streets, one that people would
really want to see.*

(Nicolas Roeg)[1]

*A plethora of camera sideswipes at chi-chi cultural
items, fed as false fodder to those who rejoice in making
pseudo-intellectual connections of no relevance to
anything . . . an overall style which plays merry hell with
chronology . . . sometimes looks like the longest
cigarette commercial ever, in the most literal sense a
drag from beginning to end.*

(John Coleman, *The New Statesman*)[2]

What is it men in women do require?
The lineaments of Gratified Desire.
What is it women do in men desire?
The lineaments of Gratified Desire.
(William Blake, 'What Is It Men in Women Do Require?')

A siren blares. A young woman Milena (Theresa Russell)
is being rushed to a hospital in Vienna, having
apparently taken an overdose of sleeping pills. With her
Theresa
Russell,
in the ambulance is Dr Alex Linden (Art Garfunkel), with
Art Garfunkel whom Milena has been having a tortured and traumatic

affair. As Milena is treated on the operating table, Dr Linden is questioned by the police, and gradually the development of their relationship is pieced together.

Structurally, of course, the film is not that simple. It jumps around in time and it is also the most densely allusive of all Roeg's films, spinning off ideas and references in all directions. One might compare it with Sir Thomas Beecham's comment on the difficulty of conducting Delius: 'The fact is that there is perhaps too much melody in Delius. When I conduct his music I turn to the wind to control a melody and behind my back, so to say, the 'cellos begin another melody. I am, in fact, *surrounded* by melody!'[3] Roeg's film too spins off lots of melodic strands, but far from being 'pseudo-intellectual connections of no relevance whatever' (John Coleman's phrase), they all feed into the atmosphere, complexity and thematic coherence of the film.

To take Coleman's simplest example, the number of cigarettes smoked in the film, which the commendably assiduous Tony Crawley has calculated as forty-seven. 'I wanted them all to smoke,' said Roeg. 'Nervousness.' Inspector Netusil (Harvey Keitel) even sniffs one fag end, but almost as an instinctive investigative reflex action: 'Is this a real cigarette, or a funny one?' as Roeg put it.[4] The smoking is a way of signalling that the film is not only about compulsive characters, but about shared, interlinked compulsions: they not only light their own cigarettes, but each other's. Similarly, it is a way of showing the impact of Milena on Alex: his obsessive tidiness breaks down as he becomes more and more caught up in Milena's messier world. The cigarettes also become crucial to the plot, because the number of Alex's cigarettes in Milena's ashtray on the night of her attempted suicide cast doubt on Alex's story about the amount of time he spent in her room. The cigarettes, then, relate to a second plot that gradually begins to take over the first, turning the film from love story almost into murder mystery: we begin to wonder not simply why this affair broke up, but what actually happened between Alex and Milena on the night of her attempted suicide.

Although Yale Udoff's screenplay is enormously intelligent and complex, structurally it might have been better if this mystery element of the plot had been stressed earlier rather than concentrating first on the mystery of character and saving the horrific revelation of Alex's behaviour as a damning denouement.

What about the implications of the film's title? There are several specific examples of 'bad timing' in the narrative. On one occasion, Milena arrives a day late at the border between Austria and Czechoslovakia to meet Alex and their subsequent argument revolves around their different attitude to time. As an extension of that, they also quarrel about being forced by your partner into being 'different from who you are'. Alex's delay in rushing Milena to the hospital, as we shall see, will prove an instance of not just bad but evil, almost murderous, timing. From the Inspector's point of view, also, the arrival of Milena's husband Stefan (Denholm Elliott) at the precise moment when the Inspector seems to have Alex on the point of confession is also unfortunate timing.

More fundamentally, the notion of 'bad timing' informs the whole relationship between Alex and Milena, whose senses of time are out of synchronization with each other and whose different attitudes to time define their personalities to some degree. Alex wishes to put the relationship on a permanent basis, an insurance for the future and not just an experience of the present. Milena, on the other hand, lives for the moment and wants a relationship that makes present time seem more vital and alive. When he proposes marriage to her in Casablanca, it hardly registers. Why can you not just respond to the moment? Feel the excitement at that particular point? Why does it have to be translated into a long-term commitment?

The complexity of the film derives, in some ways, from our attempt to mediate between, or evaluate, these two responses. Is Alex's attitude a symptom of 'normality', or of an inhibited, destructive conservatism? (There is an intriguing moment in one of his psychoanalysis lectures when he remarks that 'a guilt-ridden voyeur is usually a political conservative': he is certainly to become a guilt-ridden voyeur as the film develops.) Is Milena's attitude symptomatic of a culpable irresponsibility, promiscuity, neurosis even, or is it a laudable attempt at freedom, a refusal to be possessed as an object? Or are both attitudes symptomatic of a basic insecurity – in his case leading to a desire to *order* the future, in hers a refusal to face it? The film's tortured psychologizing and anguished sexuality is Freudian cinema with a vengeance. Mainstream film has not thrown up a bolder study of voyeurism, necrophilia and romantic perversity since Hitchcock's *Vertigo* (1958).

Just as *Don't Look Now* seems a story and a film that . could only take place in Venice (the city of death, the city of the blind, the city in, and of, peril), *Bad Timing* is a story that could only take place in Vienna – the city of Freud and Strauss, of Schnitzler and Klimt, the city of psychoanalysis and sexuality, with the scent of neurotic romanticism and the lure of decadence. (It is also, as the zither music which Alex listens to in a café reminds us, the city of *The Third Man*, already alluded to in *The Man Who Fell to Earth*: *Bad Timing* will be another dark tale of friendship betrayed.) The film opens on a shot of Gustav Klimt's painting 'The Kiss', before moving to a view of the more tortured lovers of Egon Schiele. Later Milena and Alex discuss the Klimt painting. 'They look happy,' she says, to which Alex replies: 'That's because they don't know each other well enough yet . . . Definitely happy. At least I hope so.' Roeg then cuts to Schiele. It is a movement from eroticism to anguish, a premonition of the development of the Milena-Alex relationship as they get to know each other only too well.

Given the development of this relationship, Roeg and his writer Udoff might well have been inspired by 'The Bride', an unfinished painting by Gustav Klimt, which the art critic Alessandra Commini has described as follows: 'In opposition to the floating knot of figures covering the left side of the canvas, the splayed-out nude body of a young girl dominated the other half. Her face was averted in a profile turn to the right, and a muffler-like wrap at the throat seemed to separate the head from its glimmering white torso, creating a startling effect of mutilation . . . The unknown ransackers of the studio [burglars had broken into Klimt's premises] had, sheerly by accident, caught the artist in the secret and revelatory act of flagrant voyeurism.'[5] A splayed-out nude body; something at her throat that seems more like a scar than a scarf; an effect of mutilation; a 'secret and revelatory act of flagrant voyeurism' – one could hardly be closer to the atmosphere and action of *Bad Timing*. Roeg shares with Hitchcock a belief that settings are not just there for backdrop but to be used as a crucial dramatic protagonist, as an important supporting player. He also, here as in his other work, seems fascinated with the situation of aliens in a foreign land, struggling to learn the language, experiencing difficulties of communication.

The significant action of the film is not confined exclusively to Vienna: there are, for example, important scenes that take place on the border between Austria and Czechoslovakia. Near the beginning Milena and Stefan part there; Alex goes there again around the middle of the film to meet Milena. The notion of borderlines or of crossing borders is an important metaphor in the film. It relates in a suggestive way, for example, to the situation of the two main characters: to Milena's difficulty in holding a balance between independence and commitment, self-expression and self-preservation; to Alex's difficulty in holding a balance between curiosity and obsession, trust and jealousy, between the desire to love and the desire to possess. Milena is half-married, half-divorced: the little tug-of-war with her husband at the border over her wedding ring is a finger ballet of confusion wrestling with commitment. 'To be in between is to be no place at all,' says Alex to her about her marriage; and one notes that one of the texts she has in the back of her car is Pinter's significantly entitled *No Man's Land*. Alex, on the other hand, is a man of reason and logic suddenly tempted to cross over into a world of exciting but dangerous chaos, which he can attempt to master but which might destroy him. It will lead him to a situation where he will take his relationship to an extreme point of love bordering on necrophilia as Milena lies on the border between life and death.

Gradually these borders merge, the lines between them begin to disappear. The love-making scenes and the scenes on the operating table are intercut in such a way that they seem not separate but inseparable, as if the second is the logical consequence of the first. 'Is there any hope for us, Doctor?' enquires Milena ironically of Alex about their relationship: cut to Milena, fighting for her life on the operating table. Mysterious connections slowly become apparent across the narrative. Alex fiddles with a penknife; the surgeon wields a scapel: the former becomes an instrument of his defilement of Milena and almost leads to her death; the latter saves her life. Alex is a doctor of psychology, as against the doctor of medicine: mind/body; psychological/physical. Who are the greater healers? Alex might well have taken rationalism – the desire to know being synonymous with the desire to possess, to dominate – to the point where it almost becomes a murder weapon. 'I wish you'd understand me less and love me more,' writes Milena in a note to Alex.

The desire to know brings Alex into close proximity with the Inspector. Both are investigators into motive and behaviour; psychological enquirers who are appalled yet fascinated by the worlds they uncover ('they try to drag us into their confusion, their chaos . . .' says the Inspector to Alex about women.) They both try to fathom mystery rather than accept it, and are both observers who become voyeurs: note, for example, how the Inspector's search of Milena's room is cross-cut with a flashback of a violent sexual encounter between Alex and Milena, so that it looks as if he is watching that.

At one stage, Alex gives a lecture about the child as the 'first spy', showing a slide of a child and a slide of a father and mother making love and projecting them on opposite walls. It is a neat visual idea: is the child the *product* of the act of love, or a watcher of it? It bears an interesting relationship to Alex's situation. He thinks he is the agent of investigation into human behaviour but, as the film progresses, he becomes the subject under review: the watcher becomes the watched.

Indeed the subject of spying is a *leitmotif* of the film. Alex finds himself looking through some personality profiles on behalf of American Intelligence for evidence of possible subversives and comes across files on Stefan and Milena. Is Stefan a spy? Is Milena a traitor to Alex? Or could one say that Alex betrays his profession, treating and exploiting Milena in an appalling way if she is as neurotic as he thinks? *Bad Timing* becomes a film about a lecturer in psychoanalysis who cannot acknowledge the dark forces within himself. As in Hitchcock's *Vertigo*, the hero attempts to convert the heroine into a desired image which he can control and the result is, as Jan Dawson remarks, 'to reveal the necrophiliac lurking beneath the socially acceptable form of the possessive lover.'[6] Like the Gerald-Gudrun relationship in D.H. Lawrence's great novel *Women in Love* the work develops into an intense battle of the sexes in which a man's inability to master, or overpower, the woman he desires leads to near-murder (throttling again) in a Continental setting. Gudrun's message to Gerald is almost identical to Milena's note to Alex: 'Try to love me a little more and want me a little less.'[7]

Gudrun's message goes to the heart of a key scene in *Bad Timing*. Alex has always been hostile to Milena's untidiness, wiping her cigarette ash off his car seat, complaining (as he is becoming more deeply involved with her, less in control) that 'my place is beginning to look exactly like your place.' Now she tidies up her flat, dresses conservatively and greets Alex in a friendly manner. Alex is delighted and overwhelmed, and his immediate response is to want to take Milena to bed. She politely refuses; he then becomes petulant and makes an excuse to leave; deeply upset, she follows him, shouts after him, taunts him; and he comes back to make violent love to her on the stairs.

In an article in *Sight and Sound*, John Pym suggests that Alex is 'perversely degraded' by Milena, who 'orders him to "rape" her on the stairs of her apartment building to avenge his assumption that she is *always* sexually available.'[8] Jan Dawson is surely nearer the truth when she characterizes Milena's invitation as a 'contemptuous challenge' and asserts that 'his act of animal brutality leaves her at least as degraded as himself.'[9] Pym's account omits the whole prelude to the scene which is crucial – Alex's petulant excuse for leaving when Milena does not want to make love – and also omits Milena's tragic cry after the scene: 'Love *me*, love *me*, love *me*, love *me* . . . ' It is the cry of someone who wants to be loved for herself, not possessed as a sexual object. Pym's reading seems an account in which normal man is goaded beyond endurance by a female harpy. Jan Dawson's feminist reading of the scene as a male supremacist's attempt to subjugate a woman to his own image of her seems closer to the feeling of the scene. After all, if like all Roeg's characters, the two will have been changed and marked by their experience during the film, Milena carries that mark *visibly* on her throat, the scar from her operation.

There is a later scene where Milena and Alex meet on the university grounds, and Alex begins questioning her about a man in a photograph, whom she asserts is her brother. 'What are you afraid of, Alex?' she asks, which is like the policeman's question to John Baxter in *Don't Look Now*: 'What is it . . . you fear?' Perhaps it is a fear of losing control, of venturing where he is afraid to go. 'Don't be afraid . . . I'm a friend . . . ' says Donald Sutherland in *Don't Look Now*: it is the last thing he will say, since what he thinks is his surrogate daughter is actually the murderer. It is one of the most sinister lines possible in Roeg: think of the friendship in *Performance*, and then what happens to the Aborigine who befriends the children in *Walkabout*, Newton's betrayal by his friends in *The Man Who fell to Earth*. In *Bad Timing*, Alex is asked to define his relationship to Milena and he finds it very difficult. 'A friend,' he says finally, the implication being that with friends like that . . . But it is significant that he cannot find a word to define his relationship with Milena, any more than he can define the relationship itself: not relative, not husband (because she has one), not lover (because he suspects she has so many). She does not fit into any category.

'You'll never change, Milena,' he says, 'Never.' 'If you weren't who you are, I wouldn't have to,' she replies. They are standing outside the university building and Alex is beginning to wonder about a man who is hovering around Milena, waiting: friend? new lover? It is a straightforward scene which must have looked quite simple and uneventful on paper but it is one of the best directed in the film. It could have been done in simple two-shot: reaction shot/reverse angle and so on. But first Richard Hartley's musical accompaniment is highly evocative – throbbing, rhythmic, pumping the scene with tension and vitality. Then there are brief whispered internal monologues as well as the dialogue. Moreover, Roeg's camerawork is the reverse of merely functional. In the close-up of Milena, the background is out of focus, a correlative to her feeling of imminent inner disintegration. The camera zooms towards Alex, as if impaling him, accusingly: the supposed objective psychologist, actually the jealous spy.

Inspector Netusil is now beginning to suspect something of Alex's disturbing obsession and where it might have led him. Alex's account of the time he went to Milena's flat does not square with the evidence. His car radio still tuned to a station that had finished at midnight, the clutter of cigarettes in the ashtray, the evidence of sexual penetration, all point to a different conclusion. 'Ravishment,' says the Inspector. 'You take advantage of someone's love . . . disguise your hate . . . ' At this point he makes the same gesture of spreading his hands that Alex has made earlier to Milena's question: 'How much do you love me?' The connection and contrast between the two characters is once again made evident (earlier we have seen Alex putting up an abstract print on the wall of his apartment, whilst in the next shot Netusil in his home is taking down an identical picture). Both are investigators and detectives of a different kind, which in Alex's case has led to guilt, which in turn leads to Netusil's offer to become his 'confessor', his conscience almost.

'Tell me . . . what you dare not . . . ' What Alex dare not tell is that he ravished Milena whilst she was prostrate because of the overdose. The 'ravishment' is like a thematically similar, though visually more discreet, moment in Joseph Losey's *Accident* (1967), where the don rapes the girl student, something he will have to live with for the rest of his life and which he will, on no account, be able to tell anyone. Alex has been an observer, a man who stands to one side of experience, paring his fingernails, as it were (to borrow James Joyce's image of the artist). Gradually he has become involved, overwhelmed by the dark sexual forces within him. The penknife, which he toyed with during his first meeting with Milena ('If we don't meet, there's always the possibility it could have been perfect,' he said smugly, before pursuing the relationship), now becomes an instrument of defilement as he slits Milena's clothes; the relation between the sexual act and violence – because it involves an act of penetration – is disturbingly underlined; and rational man is suddenly overcome by a side of his personality he never knew existed.

The entrance of Stefan fatally breaks the spell that Netusil is trying to cast around Alex, and the moment for confession evaporates with the news that Milena will recover. 'You must love her tremendously,' says Stefan to Alex, 'more even than one's own dignity.' But is that more revealing about him than about the woman, not a statement of female capriciousness but of male obsession? There is a dissolve, and the room, now emptied of people, is transformed from order to chaos. We see Netusil, looking at himself in a mirror, reflecting perhaps on his *doppelgänger* relationship with Alex, or even wondering about the misogyny that could lurk beneath his rational façade. (Note that the framed Harvard diploma on Netusil's wall is for athletics. 'If he had been more academic', says Reog, 'I think he would have won that struggle with Linden'.[10]) There is a brief final scene when the two former lovers see each other again. Alex calls her name and she turns – so sad, so silent – to face him, her throat bearing the scar of her relationship: in Jan Dawson's words, 'a further act of violation of the flesh to enable Milena to breathe again'.[11] There is a subliminal recollection of their first meeting ('Call me . . . '), which reinforces the trauma of what it has led to, and Alex stares desperately at her through the window of a car – as he has in the film so often. It pulls away, diminishing him before our eyes.

Roeg cuts to a last shot of the grey Danube, the calm after the storm perhaps, a reminder of earlier scenes at the border, when Stefan and Milena parted, when Alex and Milena argued and then resumed their relationship. The river is now emptied of people: impassive, oppressive, brooding, as if all passion has been spent. Over the end credits we hear the voice of Billie Holliday as she sings a love song: 'the same old story . . . of a boy and girl in love . . . but it's new to *me* . . . '

Eureka (1983)

I wanted the gold and I sought it;
I scrabbled and mucked like a slave.
Was it famine or scurvy – I fought it;
I hurled my youth into a grave.
I wanted the gold and I got it –
Came out with a fortune last fall –
Yet somehow life's not what I thought it.
And somehow the gold isn't all.

(Robert W. Service, *Spell of Yukon*)

Nature's first green is gold;
Her hardest hue to hold.
Her early leaf's a flower;
But only so an hour.
Then leaf subsides to leaf;
So Eden sank to grief.
So dawn goes down to day;
Nothing gold can stay.

(Robert Frost, 'Nothing Gold Can Stay')

Abandon preconceptions all ye who enter here.

(Nicolas Roeg)

Rutger Hauer, Gene Hackman, Theresa Russell

As the screenwriter for *Eureka* Paul Mayersberg has observed, most of the classic stories of gold-lust, like *Greed* and *The Treasure of the Sierra Madre* have ended with the loss of the gold as it blows away to dust.[1] *Eureka* is different. The hero keeps the gold, but *he* gets blown away to dust. A man who has everything, Jack

81

McCann (Gene Hackman), loses his head. It is Roeg's *Citizen Kane*, with Eureka as Xanadu, and a hero with his own Rosebud (in this case, a philosopher's stone that falls when he dies) and even a cockatoo. But McCann is not William Randolph Hearst: he is more like Orson Welles. When you have achieved your dream, your ultimate, your ecstasy, what do you do with the rest of your life? You experience a spiritual death. You die twice, which makes you hard to kill at the end, because you have been there before.

One of the things noticeable about the interviews with Roeg and Mayersberg at the time of *Eureka*'s release was the number of times that the name of Welles cropped up in their conversations, even in contexts that did not concern him particularly. 'But filmgoers have been conditioned. They expect the same sort of answers in a film: What's the plot? What happens here? I get very frustrated. But to be bitter about people not liking you – that would be a very spoilt attitude. It's like trying to force food on someone. That's something I admire very much in Welles – he never became bitter no matter what people said.'[2] If *Eureka* is a British film-maker's *Citizen Kane* – both are gigantic films about egomaniac tycoons who achieve their materialist goals too early in life and then have to discover how to live – then maybe Roeg is to the British cinema what Welles was to the American: a talent too big to contain, constantly in conflict with the economic/exhibition side of the industry.

Eureka is also a very Roegian, as well as a Wellesian, film: a 'Roeg elephant of a movie,' as *Variety* put it. Maybe McCann is Roeg to an extent: outsider, loner, obsessive. As with Turner in *Performance*, the older McCann is a recluse awaiting an intruder: his body lives on but his demon is dead. 'He needed someone to finish him off', says his daughter Tracy, 'and that night [the night of his murder], he found him, just as he found the gold.' Like Turner, like the Aborigine in *Walkabout*, like John Baxter in *Don't Look Now*, he is a character who seems to will his own death, which becomes a blood-soaked even voluptuous renunciation of the life-force. As in *Walkabout*, there is an early suicide that resonates throughout the film, that provides a foretaste of things to come. As in *Performance* there is a courtroom drama; as in *The Man Who Fell to Earth*, violent capitalist gangsters invade the hero's life because his obdurate aloofness is obstructing the flow of their greed. Although it has the obsessive sexiness of *Bad Timing*, the thing it most shares with that film is the idea of the double. Each character seems a reflection of another. Even the reclusive McCann and the gangster Mayakofsky (Joe Pesci), who never meet – and in a sense, can never meet since they inhabit two separate worlds – but who both have daughters they adore, seem flip sides of the same coin: McCann the dinosaur facing backward towards the past; Mayakofsky the developer, the man of the future.

The film begins as the camera loftily skims the mountain tops before descending to the little world of man, locked in his own conflicts and fears. A fight is taking place between McCann and his prospector partner. The latter obviously wants to give up the search for gold; McCann equally insistently wants to go on. Ice and heat: hot passions in a cold climate, as in *King Lear*. The camera zooms towards the moon, as if readying us for McCann's cosmic quest. 'I never earned a nickel from another man's sweat,' he says, three times – and he is to say it again. It is an insistence bordering on obsession: a fierce independence and isolation which, even in later life, will continue in McCann and alienate him from his new business 'partner', Charlie Perkins (Ed Lauter), a partner he neither wants nor needs and who will actually betray him.

McCann wanders into a mining town and there he encounters a barefooted prospector in front of the claims office, proclaiming: 'The end.' 'It's not over 'til it's over,' murmurs McCann. The man pays no attention and blows out his brains in a graphically gory moment. It is a moment looking ahead to McCann's similar moment later in the film of mind-blowing ecstasy, and his own death in which he loses his head. Later we see him alone in the snow, with wolves surrounding him in his lair, prowling, predatory: it will be like that in his luxury lair on the last night of his life, when Mayakofsky's wolves will be prowling around McCann's territory, searching for him to finish him off.

In the town, he visits a brothel whose housekeeper Frieda (Helena Kallianotes) is a fortune-teller with an uncanny gift. McCann has his own talisman, the stone, which becomes an elusive symbol as the film develops: all the characters are rocks, you cannot get at them; and this stone is the only thing McCann clings to, as if it holds the secret to his life. 'There was something between us that was as good as gold,' Frieda tells him. 'You'll find what you're looking for . . . but after . . . ' And he does find what he is looking for, with Wagner's 'Rheingold' music swelling in orgiastic ecstasy as the screen is suffused with the colour gold. But Roeg crosscuts the scene of McCann's triumph with the collapse of his love, Frieda, as if the two are intimately connected. As indeed they are: the *price* of his strike will be the death of Frieda, the death of that capacity for love in him, that tenderness, the rosebud in him. When he returns to her, it is too late for them both and, in a sense, too early for him. 'What happens now?' he asks. 'A mystery . . . ' is the reply. The film's first title was *Murder Mystery*.

A cinder falls from a fire, a spark flies, and suddenly the story has been sent forward seventeen years, from 1925 to 1942. We are in a new era. 'It's as if', said Mayersberg, 'his story began before there were humans, and ends after the humans have all gone from the world'.[3] McCann is sitting in the snow by a campfire with his daughter Tracy and we learn in conversation that she has fallen in love with and married a French playboy Claude (Rutger Hauer) of whom McCann strongly disapproves. From cosmic openings, the film is now shifting ground into an intense family saga, in which love of father for daughter will also be translated into hatred of son-in-law. 'I *want* him,' says Tracy. Her ecstasy echoes her father's but she finds it not in gold itself but in a golden-haired man, her Golden Boy. No doubt, she will be as let down, disillusioned, exhausted when the ecstasy has been fulfilled and she has nowhere left to go. In the meantime, her father is jealous. He and daughter are linked by his present of a golden chain, which ties them together like an umbilical cord. Claude will later contemptuously accuse McCann of raping the earth and stealing gold; McCann will see Claude's taking of his daughter in the same way, accusing him of stealing part of his flesh. We are back in the atmosphere of the first scene: hot emotions in cold climate. A cinder falls, and suddenly the frozen McCann is reignited, by jealousy, which will spread like a forest fire and find him ultimately consumed in flames. From here until McCann's death, nearly every scene will seem to end with either the threat of murder, or the potential for murder, or the atmosphere of murder.

What follows is a scene in which Roeg's and Mayersberg's elliptical, telescopic style is seen at its most dazzling. The surface content deals with Claude and Tracy in love on a yacht, but being watched through a telescope by McCann, whilst McCann's business partner is trying to interest him in a property development deal with Mayakofsky. McCann's wife (Jane Lapotaire), meanwhile, is passing the time with a Tarot pack. Roeg weaves in and out of these characters, focusing on tiny traits and tics: McCann's jealousy, Claude's narcissism, the wife's drunken myopia, the partner's sweaty exasperation. Everything in the scene essentially revolves around McCann: an island unto himself but now at the edge of eternity and under siege, from everyone and everything. 'You don't want your fortune told,' McCann says to his wife, 'you've got a fortune.' But the Tarot pack links the wife with McCann's earlier fortune-telling mistress, Frieda. McCann does not believe in luck and does not want or need anything, but they all seem to want something from him: his wealth, his secret, even perhaps his soul. 'Weren't we in love on that ship?' says his wife to McCann, recalling earlier, happier times together: cut to the young lovers on the boat, who are now discovering romance and ecstasy, following in the McCanns' footsteps. At this point the film seems to be about the painfulness of the transition from one generation to the next. One thinks of

The Leopard: 'A man . . . can consider himself still young till the moment comes when he realizes that he has children old enough to fall in love. The Prince felt old age come over him in one blow . . . '[4]

McCann is being assailed on all sides. A scene at the dinner table ends up as a sort of Mad Hatter's Tea Party, when Claude's bumptious behaviour leads McCann to order him from the house and comment 'I won't rest until I see that man dead.' A physical, as distinct from spiritual, threat is coming from the gangster Mayakofsky who is planning to launch a casino on the island and is finding McCann's obstructive attitude very trying to his patience. 'Who is he now?' he says of McCann as he looks at pictures of his adversary. It is a telling question since McCann, like a number of other Roeg protagonists, seems to have an increasingly nebulous grip on his own identity. The menace represented by Mayakofsky can be measured by the increasing alarm of McCann's partner, Charlie Perkins, who starts carrying a golden gun. Mayakofsky wants what McCann has, but as the latter says to Charlie: 'You're frightened some guy's trying to break into my house. I'm frightened some guy's trying to break into my life.'

Roeg plays off the conflict between external and internal tensions, in much the way that Richard Lester used the television shots of Vietnam in *Petulia* (1968) to amplify the idea of violence in late 60s America feeding into people's souls. In *Eureka*, if Mayakofsky represents the physical threat to McCann, wanting his possessions, Claude is the more insidious threat, wanting his daughter and his soul. There is a war going on, which is heard on the radio and alluded to in the dialogue ('The day *Gone With the Wind* opens in Paris, the war will be over, and we shall have won . . . ') But McCann is oblivious to the war outside: he is fighting a war within his house, within his head. He is fighting his own private war, one that will eventually force Tracy to choose between father and husband and send her father a letter of farewell.

It is this that tips McCann over the edge. He bursts into

the bedroom of Tracy's and Claude's home, disturbs the naked lovers and, behaving like an angry Old Testament God, expels the corrupted young lovers from Eden. 'You want *me*,' he shouts at Claude, 'you want my *soul*,' going for him with a meat-cleaver. 'I never made a nickel from another man's sweat,' he shouts, and suddenly, as Roeg's subliminal cut-back indicates, he is back at the prospectors' tent where the film started, fighting with his partner, screaming, 'Say it loud so another man in heaven can hear you' and taking on all comers in his cosmic quest. Has anything changed, then? Is he not back where he started, a man who 'once had it all' but now 'just has everything'?

When returning home, McCann passes a poster for Chaplin's *The Gold Rush*. Very apposite: the film is being reissued at that time in 1942, but was originally issued in 1925, the year McCann struck gold. It prompts an odd recollection of the Chaplin poster in *Don't Look Now*. McCann's situation seems somewhat Chaplinesque at that point: one against the many, fearful of being attacked by the rapacious wolves beginning to gather round his door.

The tension is building. Claude and a friend from the British warship HMS Trelawny take two girls on a night out that turns into a native orgy, ecstasy here tipping over into degeneracy. This jungle orgy in the midst of civilization is perhaps another link with *Citizen Kane*, specifically with the scene where Kane sits like an ancient potentate in his tent and seems oblivious to a woman's screams (is it a rape?) heard outside. 'You must not breathe a word to anyone, ever,' says Claude to the terrified girls, when he takes them back to their ship after the orgy: like Alex's ravishment of Milena in *Bad Timing*, it is a revelation of the Dionysiac and the demonic that lurks beneath mankind's civilized, rational exterior and that erupts frighteningly and cannot be spoken of or confronted without shame or inner disintegration.

In the meantime, Mayakofsky's gangsters are trying to make McCann see reason. 'I see reason,' he says. 'I see reason everywhere. I call it greed.' Earlier he has said to his partner: 'I've been waiting for this, Charlie, a long time . . . a long, long time . . . ' Like other Roeg heroes, he seems to be willing his own death. On his way from the meeting, he spots Claude in the shadows, clearly expecting him to be there with the others, closing for the kill. When he returns to Eureka, a stone flies out of the darkness and cracks him on the head. 'You can do better than that, pardner!' he shouts back and hurries inside. The gates have a 'No Trespassing' sign, like Kane's Xanadu, but it is too late: the ground invasion has begun.

The murder scene is quite extraordinary. Roeg refers to it as the 'Night of the Fury, the rage of death, the Ides of March'.[5] The music playing is 'Roses of Picardy', but the emotions are bestial. Mayakofsky's henchmen are there, but so too are Claude and Charlie Perkins, building mystery upon planned murder – for who threw the first stone and who will strike the final blow? They stalk around his lair, like the wolves earlier in the film. The killing itself is ferocious and almost unbearably brutal, for McCann is a Colossus and takes a lot of killing. The scene reminds one of Losey's superb staging of the murder of Trotsky in *The Assassination of Trotsky* (1972), and Roeg seems to have taken some visual inspiration from that: the murder as a sort of bullfight, with the bull fatally wounded but refusing to go down. 'I knew it would be you,' McCann says enigmatically to the unseen assailant who strikes the final blow: it is his 'et tu, Brute'.

McCann dies and, at that point, so does the film. It is an awkwardly structured movie, to suggest an awkwardly structured life, like that of most people: climax followed by anticlimax, building to climax again, but then trailing to anticlimax. Having discovered the gold in middle age and then having lived on, McCann's story neither has the romanticism that might have accrued had he achieved his goal early (could he live up to it?) or the satisfying resolution that would have occurred if he had found his goal late, giving a sense of completion to his life, rounding it off. McCann just goes on living: the gold has not brought him fulfilment. Mayersberg quotes a comment by W.B. Yeats as the inspiration for this aspect of the film: life as a preparation for something that never happens.

Yet the sense of dwindling returns that characterizes the latter part of the movie cannot be entirely explained in dramaturgical terms, as a means of reflecting McCann's disillusioned development and ultimate descent. After all, the film could now turn into a whodunit, a speculative mystery along the lines of Michael Radford's *White Mischief* (1987). What it does, however, is turn into a rather tiresome courtroom drama, in which Claude is being tried for McCann's murder. When Claude suspects that Tracy has committed infidelity with Mayakofsky's lawyer, D'Amato (Mickey Rourke), he becomes disillusioned with the legal system and decides to conduct his own defence.

In the cross-examination of Tracy by Claude, public trial becomes private communion, and what is being tried is no longer the crime so much as the people themselves. Like the big courtroom dramas in David Lean's movies, *Madeleine* (1950) and *A Passage to India* (1984), the trial proves inconclusive, more a verdict of 'not proven' than 'not guilty', so Claude is sentenced to deportation rather than death. Like McCann's life, the trial of his murderer has an awkward structure: interrupted by change of lawyer, then disrupted by the news that the war is over, which seems to diminish the importance of these events. The problem for the film is that it becomes overtly rhetorical, so that Roeg seems more or less to fall asleep behind the camera. The cross-examination becomes just an inflated domestic spat between Tracy and Claude, which reduces the suspense of the story, strains credulity that a judge would actually have allowed this, and alienates us still further from two increasingly unsympathetic characters. 'For the first hour I thought it one of the best pictures ever,' John Boorman has written. 'The movie faltered when it suddenly switched from telling its story in a series of searing vivid images to courtroom drama.'[6] At this juncture the film seems to be leaning too heavily on its original source material, Marshall Houts's book, *Who Killed Sir Harry*

Oakes?, which was more about the murder trial surrounding the death of the person who was Roeg's inspiration for McCann – Sir Harry Oakes – than about the character himself. It tries to dig into areas other than the whole question of identifying the killer, but only does so at the cost of alienation: who *cares* who killed Jack McCann?

Yet this last part is not without interest. 'He was like a man struck by lightning,' says Tracy at the trial about her father's discovery of the gold. 'He was just waiting to be struck down.' The murder scene has caught that feeling superbly, the raging storm playing its full part in the elemental drama that unfolds inside McCann's Eureka, and his head. The cross-examination is important because one can feel, through Tracy's pent-up exasperation, the incipient stages of her disillusionment with Claude, whom she thought the key to her fulfilment: just as her father had done with the gold. While waiting for the verdict, Claude reads Samuel Butler's *Erewhon* in prison, a deceptive Utopian fantasy whose title is 'Nowhere' spelt backwards. As Claude's acquittal is announced, the courtroom picture of McCann's disembodied head passes across our, and Claude's vision, as if in mute but persistent accusation. Now free, Claude seems strangely rudderless: where will he go? 'Maybe back to France. See *Gone With the Wind* in Paris,' he tells Tracy. Leaving their room, he walks past a mirror and becomes aware of his own reflection. He leans his head on it (as if putting his head on the block) before murmuring McCann's last words: 'I knew it would be you.' An admission of guilt, for how else could he have heard these words? A haunted character, who might have killed McCann but who feels his presence on the dark side of that mirror – his own soul – more powerfully than ever. McCann has won. In the last shot, watched sadly by Tracy, Claude drifts away on a boat, still searching for his Eureka, whilst over the end credits, as in *Walkabout*, we have a poem that summarizes the film's theme (an extract from Robert W. Service's 'Spell of the Yukon'). The poem can be taken to represent McCann's voice beyond the grave as he reflects on the ruthless, wretched and restless survivors: 'It's the stillness that fills me with peace.' His soul is at rest.

Eureka was so hated by its distributors that they were reluctant to let it out even to cinemas that wanted it. Prefacing a recent screening of the film on BBC television, both Roeg and Mayersberg offered their opinions on the film's abject box office failure and to its drastically limited release. Mayersberg felt it was disliked so much because it was saying things that were unacceptable within the ideology of commercial American film: namely, that endeavour seemed to be a curse and victory a disaster. In an Anthony Mann Western, for example, the hero sets himself a goal and the film dramatizes the difficulties he encounters in achieving that goal, and the determination he shows in overcoming them. In *Eureka*, the hero sets himself a goal which he achieves, but then finds it may not be what he wanted. This is not a tragedy with an uplifting ending, like, say *One Flew Over The Cuckoo's Nest* (1975). This is a success story with a tragic ending, like *Citizen Kane* again. For Roeg, the explanation for the hostility to the film was, he felt, something to do with the spirit of the time. The early 1980s was a period of rampant conservatism and materialism: who wanted, or could comprehend, the story of a man who had made such a spectacular success but was not happy?

No doubt these factors were also exacerbated by the film's oblique style, in which Roeg's former narrative drive (in movies like *Walkabout* and *Don't Look Now*) seemed to disperse itself in montage particles that pulled the film sideways or upwards more than forwards. It is a film that is hard to take in. It is also a film that is often hard to take, both for the ferocity of its imagery (notably in the murder scene, but also the suicide at the beginning and the orgy) and the abrasiveness of its characterization (the young lovers are so nastily narcissistic, though there is no doubting the towering performance of Gene Hackman as McCann – in Hackman's hands, a King Lear of the Yukon). It is still a film of vaunting ambition, scintillating intellect and dazzling technique, a truly modern tragedy about the emptiness of materialism, the failure of success, gold as base metal.

Insignificance (1985)

To me the characters were mythic, not invented by any single person, not the public or the press, probably not even by the characters themselves. Familiar but strange, living or dead people made up from stories, fictions, gossip. Truly fictional people, but their fiction was made up of so many other fictions that they could represent something to everyone.

(Nicolas Roeg[1])

Insignificance *is about everything . . .*

(Publicity brochure)

New York, 1953. An Actress is being filmed with her skirt billowing up above her knees, watched by her jealous Baseball Player husband. Elsewhere a professor is being interrogated in his hotel room by a Senator who is investigating possible Communist affiliations lurking in the Professor's background. Later the actress will escape and come to the Professor's hotel room to explain to him his own Theory of Relativity. She will be followed by her jealous husband. As morning dawns, the Senator will also re-enter with his subpoena. Any resemblance to persons living or dead is purely intentional – it is part of the story.

Terry Johnson's play, *Insignificance* was first performed at the Royal Court in 1982, with Judy Davis in the role of the Actress. It was partially inspired by a knowledge that a signed photograph of Albert Einstein had been found among Marilyn Monroe's possessions

Michael Emil,
Theresa
Russell

after her death. 'It was always meant to be a play about the era, about fame', said Johnson, ' . . . what these people stood for, the fact that this was different from what they are.'[2] In changing the stage play into a screenplay, Johnson first abbreviated and then, encouraged by Roeg, re-thought it laterally. 'Take the image of the watches,' he said. 'There are two watches in the play, there are about half-a-dozen in the film. One scoured the histories of the characters and thought "watch" and various ideas presented themselves. It was a liberating way to work, though I'd have been terrified to do it without a solid structure of beginning-middle-end.'[3]

For Roeg, part of the appeal of the material, he said, was its 'detachedness' and its 'iconography'. There was also a very personal response; he was especially moved by the relationship between the Actress and the Ballplayer, the lack of communication between them, and her consequent search for someone who would listen to her impartially. 'Good God,' he remembers thinking, 'nobody knows a damn thing about anyone . . .'[4] The theme of fame is an elaboration of that. There is a split between the characters' images and the real people behind those façades. There is also a split between their insistent self-importance and their lack of self-knowledge, very dangerous in people with such power. In that context, said Roeg, what he was groping towards was a feeling that 'people would be better if they cultivated a sense of wonder . . . a sense of their own insignificance in the scheme of things . . . ' The nuclear sub-theme – the Professor's horrified memory of the Nagasaki bomb and his conception of the future conflagration that could be a consequence of his scientific discoveries – is also an extension of that. A sense of wonder, a less arrogant outlook on experience, might have prevented, or cautioned against, such an act. 'One of the aspects that I wanted to get over', said Roeg, 'was that time doesn't diminish the scale of the act.'[5]

Insignificance is Roeg's first film adaptation of a play (though he did photograph a marvellous film version of

Pinter's *The Caretaker*) and his approach is revolutionary. He opens it out not so much spatially as laterally. In Johnson's words, 'he opened it backwards.' With the word 'watch', for instance, Roeg uses it to generate images, and it begins to give off powerful visual and verbal associations. A watch is seen swinging through space. The Actress borrows her chauffeur's watch to use as part of her demonstration to the Professor of her understanding of the Theory of Relativity. A watch is also a key prop in one of the Actress's flashbacks to her childhood, when a watch is taken from her, and in a scene in a restaurant in which the Ballplayer gives her a watch as a present. Perhaps most significant is the Professor's watch, which is permanently stuck at 8.15, the time at which the bomb went off in Nagasaki, since when time for the Professor has, in a sense, stood still.

But 'watch' means something else as well. The Actress is being *watched* in the opening scene: she is the object of everyone's gaze, and the price she has to pay for her fame is the difficulty of avoiding the public stare. The word expands into the political arena too. In the paranoid atmosphere of the McCarthyist era, everyone is being *watched*, put under surveillance. Outside the hotel is a neon sign which we never see completely but which seems to overlook events as tirelessly as Dr Eckleburg's glasses in *The Great Gatsby*, for it never goes off. Contrast that with the Actress: 'I wish they'd switch me off.' In picking on the word 'watch', then, and allowing his visual imagination to work on it, Roeg has generated for himself a rich vein of fresh imagery around the main themes: time and fame. 'Because of being famous', the Professor complains, 'everywhere I go people fall over themselves to be with me, like a troupe of clowns chasing an old automobile. Because of fame, everything I do develops into a ridiculous comedy.' The Actress replies: 'You're lucky. Everything I do develops into a nightmare. People keep throwing themselves in front of me and I daren't stop.'

To take two other examples: 'fan' and 'star'. 'Fan' relates to the industrial *fan* machine being used to make the Actress's skirt billow above her knees. But, in another sense, the Actress is herself a fan machine, an industrial commodity constructed for popular public consumption. Then the word 'star' – 'She there?' asks one of the electricians in charge of the fan machine, wondering if his partner can see anything. 'You can't see nothing?' 'Just the stars,' replies his partner. The pun here is on human stars and on heavenly stars, a confusion compounded when, after the fan machine has had the desired effect and his partner asks him what he saw, the electrician replies, smilingly: 'I saw the face of God.' Later, however, the Professor and the Actress, both stars in their own field, will look out of the hotel window at the heavens and get a sense of their human insignificance. 'Stars are too far away,' says the Actress. 'They make me feel small and lonely.' 'Me too,' replies the Professor. 'All who look feel small and lonely as the rest. Doesn't that make you feel better?' The film has pirouetted elegantly on a single word – 'star' – and the emanations from that single idea have touched on key issues to do with fame, and human power and also to do with a sense of the infinite.

Like all of Roeg's films, *Insignificance* is about a group of personalities, whose identities have been shaken and even transformed by the end of the film. It concerns in particular four powerful figures, with a deep fissure between their public image and their private reality. In his blunt, unsophisticated way, the Ballplayer alludes to this when he talks about the Actress's being 'all bright lights on the outside' whereas 'inside she'd tear up if she fell down in the street.' The Senator is a bully but also impotent; the Ballplayer is known all over the world but is deeply insecure; the Professor knows everything but the burden of having seen it all is becoming too much to bear and his knowledge will be tossed out of the window like so much waste paper. These are powerful figures but pressurized figures as well. They are hemmed in by their fame. All of them are haunted by their past, not only by their upbringing which has helped shape their destiny, but also by a sense of power that is perverting or deforming their development in different ways. It is one of the farcical ironies, yet also disturbing tragedies, of their situation. In their particular fields, they are all at that stage 'at the centre of the universe', but the result is to make them feel paranoid, insecure, troubled and impotent. 'Wherever you're taking me, I don't want to go,' the Actress says to her chauffeur at one stage. She could, though, be addressing her fame, her power, which is pulling her in an undesired direction toward an unnerving destination; and her comment could equally be echoed by the other three characters. At that stage in their lives, none of them is any longer in full control of his or her destiny. They have been immortalized and aggrandized, but they have also, significantly, been flattened into two dimensions rather than three — the Actress on a calendar, the Ballplayer on a bubble-gum card, the Professor with his theses, the Senator with his subpoenas. Interestingly, and even more extremely than the four main characters of *The Man Who Fell to Earth*, all of them are introduced *alone*, profoundly isolated.

Other Roegian characteristics assert themselves. It is a film full of allusion and reference. In the case of the Actress, the film in which she is appearing is plainly *The Seven-Year Itch* — and, of course, the break up of Monroe's marriage to Di Maggio was also occurring at that time. One cause was reputedly Di Maggio's outrage at this particular skirt-blowing scene and the public pandemonium caused by it. On top of that was his general sense of alienation and shock at Marilyn's stardom and at the exhibitionist character of her roles. A more covert allusion is to *Some Like it Hot*, where Tony Curtis's Senator tries to cure his impotence with a Marilyn lookalike. More esoteric are the books in the Professor's hotel. One of them is Dostoevsky's *The Brothers Karamazov*, the most apocalyptic of nineteenth-century novels, which at one stage debates the proposition that, if God is dead, then everything is permitted: *Insignificance* takes place in what looks like a godless universe in which the permitted has become the perverted. Yet Dostoevsky also said that, if you could prove his work caused the death of a single child, then it should all be burnt. The Professor in *Insignificance* is wrestling with the same problem. 'We burned children,' he says to the Actress in a whisper, talking of the fear and guilt that preoccupy him. 'You're not responsible for that,' she says. 'You don't believe you're responsible for that. Not for that.' But what if he is, and what if his scientific genius gives rise to something even worse?

The other book that is visibly prominent on the Professor's shelves is *Jane Eyre*, which is also, like *Insignificance*, about an oppressed heroine searching for independence, about a struggle between reason and passion, and a tale that oscillates fascinatingly between reality, myth, and elemental extremes. 'Looking up, I, with tear-dimmed eyes, saw the mighty Milky Way,' says Jane at a low point in her career. It could be the Actress in Roeg's movie, pondering her insignificance in the scheme of things.

The style is unmistakably Roeg, from visual motifs such as flying glass or visual signatures such as the use of slow motion or the use of violence to deliver a blow that seems to reach to the pit of your stomach: the Senator's savage punch at the Actress's pregnant belly, which will bring on her miscarriage, is shocking even by Roeg's standards. Also unmistakable is Roeg's lateral-thinking montage that seems triggered by mental association more than narrative linearity. 'You philosophical fucking genius' says one electrician ironically to the other: cut to the Professor as he paces his hotel bedroom. 'You strike me as the movie-star type, the kind that mud sticks to,' says the Senator to the Professor: cut to the actress as she walks into the all-night store.

Like *The Man Who Fell to Earth*, *Insignificance* is a film about space and about time; the treatment is both airy and apocalyptic. Like *Don't Look Now*, the film is a mixture of tragedy and farce. (Roeg's comment was that 'I hope that *Insignificance* is a Real, Mythical, Melodramic Farce'.[6]) On the one hand, it considers nuclear annihilation, the permanent 'dying of the light', guilt, marital break-up, political persecution, the death of children, both individually (the Actress's miscarriage) and globally, and it thinks of time running out, of our fears for the future – a fear, like the Professor's, either of thinking back or of moving time forward. Yet, on the other hand, it is also a farce. It is about trousers falling down, manic knocks on the door, hiding in the bathroom, unexpected people turning up in your bed. Pricelessly, it is about a moment – real or imaginary? – when Einstein shows his legs to Monroe as *her* reward for explaining the Theory of Relativity to him . . .

Alongside *The Man Who Fell to Earth* and, to a lesser extent, *Eureka*, it is another odd paranoid vision of America and Americans. It is set in the 1950s and moves backward in time but it has strong resonances for the mid-1980s, at a time of the renewal of the Cold War, of the return of anti-Communist feeling in the body-politic, and of a President whose persona seems a smiling mix of a mellowing McCarthy, ageless Ballplayer and an old-time movie star. Yet the film's most uplifting moment is one in which we are suddenly transported back in time when the elevator attendant (Will Sampson) does an Indian call across the Manhattan skyline. It is a sort of parody of the ending of *How the West Was Won*, a fleeting recollection also of the disorientating but significant glimpse of the American pioneers of *The Man Who Fell to Earth*, a nice allusion furthermore to the Professor's conversational comment to the Indian in the elevator that 'all true Cherokee believe wherever they are, there is the centre of the Universe', and finally an amusing, brief glimpse of America's possible destiny but for the intervention of Christopher Columbus – or as the Ballplayer colourfully put it: 'if it wasn't for Columbus, we'd all be Indians.' Mark Twain put it somewhat differently in his great novel, *Pudd'nhead Wilson*: 'It was wonderful to find America, but it would have been more wonderful to miss it.'

In the final analysis, *Insignificance* is perhaps not as significant as some other of Roeg's films. It is his funniest film, but also, up to that point, his most conventional. It can be seen as both a retreat and an advance: a retreat in its unusual dependence on the script; an advance in its modern relevance. Mostly it can be enjoyed for its splendid performances, its delightful and ingenious playing with ideas, and as an unusual and brilliant example of the translation of play into film.

Castaway (1986)

This is Roeg at his most comprehensible, rationalizing his finer flights of imagination and technical flourish to the barest but most effective minimum . . . Oliver Reed [gives] an impeccably timed and characterized performance that any actor in the world might envy.

(Derek Malcolm, *The Guardian*)[1]

A year on a desert island with Oliver Reed sounds like the second prize in a competition in which the first prize is six months on a desert island with Oliver Reed, chaperoned by Mary Whitehouse. Still, that is what the heroine of Castaway *gets; . . . and I didn't give a damn about its self-exiled duo and the pain of their self-inflicted wounds.*

(Philip French, *The Observer*)[2]

No voice divine the storm allay'd,
No light propitious shone;
When, snatch'd from all effectual aid;
We perish'd, each alone;
But I beneath a rougher sea;
And 'whelm'd in deeper gulfs than he'.

(William Cowper, 'The Castaway')

Amanda Donohoe, Oliver Reed Roeg's film *Castaway* is based on Lucy Irvine's book about her year on a desert island with Gerald Kingsland. It also takes cognizance of Kingsland's counter-version of events in his book, *The Islander*. It sets out the situation concisely over the opening credits.

A small ad is being placed in the appropriate column of the magazine *Time Out*, which is in turn an appropriate name for what is being proposed: 'time out' from their mundane lives. The ad will finally read: 'Writer, 35+ seeks "wife" for year on tropical island.' However, we have watched the ad being composed and that final version includes two significant modifications from the original. '45' has been changed to '35+', which is perhaps a tiny hint of Kingsland's vanity. More significantly quotation marks have been placed around the word 'wife'. It is an odd reminder of a detail in *Citizen Kane*, when the newspapers proclaim that Kane (Orson Welles) has been caught in a love nest with a 'singer', and his former friend Leland suggests that Kane's whole attempt to establish his wife Susan as an opera star could be read as an egocentric attempt to erase those quotation marks from the word 'singer'. That detail in *Castaway* has a similar kind of importance, and indeed can be seen to encapsulate the tension of the whole relationship between Kingsland and Irvine. He, in a sense, wants to wipe out the quotation marks surrounding the word 'wife': she wants to keep them in. Because of this, what develops is another Lawrentian tug-of-war between a 'male chauvinist pig' and a cocksure feminist. The man tries to achieve dominance: the woman – articulate, intelligent, elusive, obscure – refuses to accept submission.

Described like this, the movie sounds like another rake over *Bad Timing* territory. The isolated setting as a metaphor for man and woman's essential isolation might also be seen as analogous to *Walkabout*. Reviewing the film in the *Monthly Film Bulletin*, Pam Cook was immediately struck by the similarity to *Don't Look Now*[3]: the flight from a horrific existence to an ostensible paradise that turns out to be a nightmare; the study of a couple seeking an unattainable ideal; the imagery that links water and desire with death and menacing undercurrents. It is another Roeg study of characters in a foreign land whose relationship disintegrates. Indeed, it is easy to identify *Castaway* as a Roeg film – it is very much an *auteurist* film – but at the same time the movie does not resonate quite so powerfully as the best of Roeg.

The action of the film begins with an evocation of the London lives of the two leading characters, clearly aiming to establish the reasons for their wanting to escape (in the way that the opening of *Walkabout* aims obliquely to suggest an atmosphere in which the father's desire for oblivion, for self-destruction, seems plausible.) Lucy (Amanda Donohue) works for the Inland Revenue, shares a flat with a friend, has friends but no steady boyfriend, it seems: and, to judge from the brief office scene and the ogling men, is subject to niggling sexual harassment at work. Gerald (Oliver Reed) is a swimming instructor, with two teenage sons. As he is going home one evening, he sees in a shop window a model of an island. This scene evokes for us both his dreams of escape and (because he is framed in the reflection of the window) his feeling of being trapped as in a goldfish bowl.

'Of course, I could make a film in the realist or social tradition,' Roeg has said. 'It would not be me and I could only do it once. People would see through it.'[4] The opening section of *Castaway* is something of a departure for Roeg, his gesture towards social realism. On the evidence of this, he might yet make his Ken Loach film. How crisply, and yet also how satirically, he evokes the leery atmosphere of the office where Lucy works, the oafish camaraderie of Gerald's pub pals, the jostle of London. The atmosphere is filled out with a concentrated counterpoint of media sensationalism. The Yorkshire Ripper reports on TV contend for attention with royal romance between Charles and Diana, whilst the tabloids have headlines that scream out such nuggets as 'Sex Swap Father is a Mother Now' and 'How I Escaped Rapist Curate': prurience, violence, Ruritanian romance set against sexual harassment. The banal horror of modern life, its irredeemable decadence and irreligion (the shooting of the Pope is another TV highlight), suffice to show why Lucy and Gerald would wish to escape. Also, in evoking the idea of sexual threat, it shows why Lucy would prefer to be Gerald's 'wife' rather than his real wife – it at least keeps the male at arm's length.

The allusions to the royal wedding are interesting. On the one hand, the fairy-tale romance between Charles and Diana contrasts with the sleazy sexuality of, for example, the tabloids. But it also connects with the Lucy-Gerald relationship in an oblique way – an arranged marriage that has nevertheless the promise of fantasy fulfilment. In a sense, the desert island retreat represents the idea of marriage in our culture which the royal wedding blows up to its fullest proportions – romantic release, paradisal fulfilment, perennial blue skies, the ultimate dream of happiness, all of which might be a long way removed from reality. (It is a disgruntled, sexually frustrated Gerald who will brutally yoke all these ideas together, in so doing stripping them of all romanticism and glamour, when he talks of his desire for Lucy 'flat on your back . . . being given one . . . like some members of the royal family'). What will happen is that the desert-island experience will in a sense compress a lifetime's marriage into one year of combustible marital breakdown; or alternatively will be a portrait of a honeymoon hideously protracted to unendurable lengths leaving the wedded couple exhausted, alienated and, in almost every way, incompatible.

Something of this is foreshadowed in the first telephone conversation between Gerald and Lucy, which takes place while both happen to be watching Jack Clayton's *The Pumpkin Eater* (1964) on television. It is one of Roeg's most eloquent uses of film quotation. At first the marital row taking place in the film between Anne Bancroft and Peter Finch seems a premonition of the marital battles to come between Gerald and Lucy. But the analogies are rather more extensive and suggestive than that. For example, we glimpse an earlier scene at a zoo where a cuckolded James Mason becomes threatening towards Anne Bancroft: a portrait of predatory *human* nature of a kind that both surrounds and unnerves Lucy at home – notice that strange moment when she draws a red mark on her body when watching reports on the Yorkshire Ripper on television – and will begin to oppress her on the island. 'You live in a dream world, you know that?' snaps Peter Finch at Anne Bancroft during their row: at that point, Gerald is looking at his fish tank in his room and dreaming of exotic escape, which might not be as much of an escape as he imagines. 'I wish you'd shut up,' continues Finch, 'I wish you'd die!' Love/Death, Marriage/Possession – we are quite close here to the world of *Bad Timing*. 'I could die here', says Anne Bancroft. Roeg chooses to handle that line as a kind of dying fall to his scene in *Castaway*, not shown but half heard by Lucy as she replaces the receiver, almost as a voice in her own subconscious. Lucy almost could, metaphorically speaking, 'die here'. She must get away to live.

The first meeting between Gerald and Lucy and a subsequent scene at a restaurant hint at the developments to come. Gerlad describes their encounter as 'the ultimate blind date' but, although there is clearly an attraction between them, his chauvinism and her feminism rub incongruously against each other in the restaurant scene. It has humour, tension, small false starts and misunderstandings that seem a prelude in miniature for the storms ahead. 'Give me a woman that can cook, sew, put up a tent, fish . . . ' begins Gerald, only gradually getting to companionship. 'In that order?' asks Lucy, amused, but he does not pick up on her irony. She has to check Gerald's reveries about Robinson Crusoe by pointing out that 'he had a Friday as well'. They pick an island, Tuin, off the northern coast of Australia.

There are certain personality differences, then, which suggest that their experience might well prove not to be as idyllic as anticipated. The setting, by removing all the trappings and essentials that cushion our civilization, has the effect of throwing the characters back on their naked selves and hence highlighting these differences still further, since they cannot be hidden. But even before they get to the island, certain clouds have appeared on the horizon, notably the requirement by the immigration laws that they get married first. Lucy at first rebels and is prepared to abandon the idea. She starts listening to a record of Pavarotti as he sings Puccini's 'Nessun Dorma' from *Turandot* – the needle significantly gets stuck in a groove, as she is. She then agrees to go ahead but the shackles of the marriage around her are clearly an inhibition to her sense of both emotional and sexual freedom. Indeed, although the film does not spell this out, there is an implication that marriage to Gerald is precisely the thing that turns her off the idea of having sex with him on the island. She feels that she has been trapped into marriage. Submitting to Gerald would be a loss of freedom that would negate the whole experience of going to the desert island. It would simply be enslavement in a different setting.

'They embark on their adventure,' says the critic Philip French, 'as if preparing for an appearance on *Desert Island Discs* rather than existence on a real desert island.'[5] Their unpreparedness is, of course, part of the point. As Roeg said about the couple in *Don't Look Now*, 'they were unprepared in life: most people are, aren't they?'[6] In *Castaway* he indicates this unpreparedness early on by his use of music in the wedding ceremony at the registry office. It is not Mendelssohn or Wagner, but Eric Coates and 'Sleepy Lagoon', that is, the theme for *Desert Island Discs*. Lucy is sulky and Gerald is very apologetic and soon the word 'sorry' becomes one of their commonest dialogue exchanges.

On the island their relationship rapidly deteriorates. Even their ecstatic arrival is modified by the presence of a media photographer, turning seclusion into an event, and the photographer's black helper, who Gerald notices with some disgust taking a pee amongst the island foliage, thoughtlessly despoiling their Eden. Still Lucy is naked and Gerald runs up expectantly, only to be checked by Lucy's invitation: 'Tea?' It is *Brief Encounter* on a desert island: make tea, not love. As in *Walkabout*, and his other films, Roeg will feature a lot of nakedness in *Castaway*, but as embarrassment or provocation more than eroticism.

As Philip French has noted, many of Roeg's films are about people away from home whose relationships go awry (another link with Lean, in whose films the concept of 'home' is often nebulous, mysterious, even menacing). Lucy finds Gerald disorganized and forgetful, and her irration at this makes her reject Gerald's first request for love-making: he has forgotten to bring the flour and the iodine. He in turn finds her shrewish — he has to suffer something like a nagging wife without the compensation of gratified desire. Part of the interest as the relationship develops is the way it seems to evoke so many archetypal partnerships, as he at times plays Adam to her Eve, Petruchio to her Kate, Crusoe to her Friday and even (in his rough diamond exterior and her forbidding femininity) Bogart to her Hepburn. One is reminded a little of *The African Queen* in Gerald's occasionally lackadaisical attitude and his mechanical skill, and in Lucy's stern disapproval and equally stubborn determination. 'I once read Izaak Walton's *Compleat Angler*,' she says as part of a grumble about Gerald's aimless fishing. 'It was incredibly boring'. 'What did you read it for, then?' asks Gerald. 'Because', she replies, 'I never give up once I've started'.

Roeg amplifies the themes and tensions with an array of striking imagery. Rocks stand out like fists on the smooth sands, a correlative to Gerald's masculine hardness against Lucy's softer sensuality. Lucy writhes naked amongst the ferns in a Lawrentian agony of sexual anger and frustration, like Birkin in *Women in Love*. Gerald stares at an emaciated impaled bird in a tree, a prisoner on the isle of freedom, a scarecrow: it is an omen of their own state of emaciation and malnutrition to come. Lucy drapes herself underneath a blue veil, in a scene in which Gerald almost loses control, kissing her violently before drawing away. Is there something about Lucy's teasing sexuality that invites violence, which she might sense and which might be why she seems so uneasy when watching the Yorkshire Ripper reports on TV? She seems like the archetypal 'cocksure' woman: intelligent, articulate but incomplete, unfulfilled, no woman. That is the way a man like D.H. Lawrence would look at it. Is this Roeg's view too? Lucy Irvine did say she was a little perturbed by the distribution of sympathies in the film. 'Castaway, the film', she said, 'has been made from the man's point of view – Gerald is so lovable. But I don't mind. I would rather have it that way. I wanted people to like Gerald. In the film it is he who goes off to the other side of the island and Lucy who cries because she has been left alone. But it wasn't Gerald who went off, it was me. The woman in the film has been made to look weaker than the man. It's still not 21st century.'[7]

Sometimes the situation is played for comedy. 'A screw and a cold beer are the summit of my life's ambition,' says Gerald, but when Lucy brings him some food, he comments: 'Lucy, I said screw, not stew.' Arousal and appetite are particularly the subject of a scene where the two imagine the most luscious food they could have, becoming so carried away in their ecstasy of hunger that Gerald remarks: 'Lucy, that was better than sex, wasn't it?' It is Roeg's version of the famous food-eating scene in Tony Richardson's Tom Jones (1963), except that in Richardson it becomes analogous to sexual voraciousness, whereas in Roeg it becomes sexual substitute – sex in the head rather than the bed.

A turning point occurs when Gerald becomes a handyman for the nearby island of Badu and begins spending more time there than on his and Lucy's island. Previously the denial of sex has been a way of trying to keep Gerald under control, but Lucy now realizes she will have to seduce him back for the same reason or he will drift away to the island and their experiment will have failed. In a sense, she now plays Jane Eyre to his Rochester, finally feeling free to give herself on her own terms and not his. What convinces her finally of the perilous state of affairs, which would have negated the whole experience, is the time when Gerald comes home and tosses her a frozen chicken, the modern hunter returning to his lair, a grotesque parody of the paradisal primitivism that they initially embraced, and in any case (in the casual way he tosses it to her to be readied for cooking) too much like conventional marriage. The only way she can retrieve something of the initial dream and keep Gerald in thrall on the island, is by using her sexuality – as Sue Bridehead does with Jude in *Jude the Obscure* – but at the same time keeping the essential part of her self to herself.

Time Out has brought them together, but time is running out, and a hurricane is blowing through the fragile shelter the two are now sharing. In their final embrace, Lucy is holding a clock, as if aware that their ostensible paradise would always be subject to time, and that time has run out between her and Gerald at the point when the two are closer than before: another example of bad timing. But the paradise has, of course, always involved other things – stings, ulcers, malnutrition, vomiting – just as their wedded state has been more battlefield than bliss. It is a more genial example of Roeg's work than some, but still a study of people stripped to their primitive state, confronting alternative worlds, stepping out from where they are in life and floundering, wondering whether they will sink or swim.

In dramatic terms *Castaway* presents Roeg with some problems that he never entirely resolves. It is somewhat similar to Richard Lester's problem in *The Bed-Sitting Room* (1969), where the setting is essentially defined by absences. The setting in *Castaway* does not seem to give Roeg enough to go on; it does not seem to inspire him in the way that the desert did in *Walkabout*. The desert was full of life, but this island, apart from one early manifestation that scares Lucy, is empty of noises – or resonances. It is a very plaintive paradise.

The point becomes more noticeable when *Castaway* is compared with *Walkabout*. In the latter film, Roeg contrasts not only desert and civilization, nature and culture, but also Aborigine and white culture, and Aborigine and modern life. Moreover, he does it in a richly textured montage which works as both intercutting and cross-reference. There is curiously little of this in *Castaway* (and it is hardly as if the characters have forgotten what they have left behind) and what there is is peculiarly perfunctory: a brief flash of Gerald at work, or Lucy on the Tube.

Roeg and his writer Allan Scott try to vary the dramatic

texture with two major interruptions from the outside world: a visit from two Australians with a census form; and a visit from two nuns, who provide them with medicine and antibiotics to counter their 'serious malnutrition'. Yet neither episode seems very interestingly conceived or dramatized, or adds much to what we already know. The visit from the Australians precipitates further tension in the Lucy-Gerald relationship, feeding Gerald's jealousy and intensifying Lucy's anger at him for his slovenliness and for his trying to bring her down to his level. She fantasizes about attacking him with a knife and looks at herself in a mirror, as if wondering whether she is still attractive and what the partnership with Gerald has done to her. In the meantime, the one Australian, Jason (Tony Rickards), asks the other, Rod (Todd Rippon), who has flirted with Lucy: 'Tell me, did you get a bit?' It is all a bit rudimentary and laboured and takes more time to say less than, say, the weather station scene in *Walkabout*. Similarly the scene with the two nuns (Georgina Hale and Frances Barber) seems rather to work against the film than for it. Where have they come from? It seems a very convenient, contrived appearance and one that only serves to undercut our sympathy for Lucy and Gerald by reminding us of their unpreparedness and their lack of self-sufficiency. Even the book references in the film have less resonance than in other Roeg films. Gerald reads *Buddhist Scriptures*, and Lucy reads Colin Wilson's *A Criminal History of Mankind*. But so what? They are details that do not seem to lead anywhere.

The other main problem concerns the two main characters. In stressing Gerald's chauvinism against Lucy's feminism, Roeg seems to want to express something about the conflict between Man and Woman in very elemental terms. Unfortunately the archetype becomes the stereotype. Gerald is still the provider; Lucy is still represented as dependent. The sexual contrasts seem much starker and simpler than, in, say, *Bad Timing*, stripped so much to their bare essentials that development becomes almost impossible. It is not just that, for example, the scene in *Bad Timing* where tension is caused when Milena does not want to sleep with Alex comes over as a much more complex psychological conflict than that which rages between Gerald and Lucy over the same situation. It is that this problem occupies just one scene of *Bad Timing* whereas in *Castaway* it seems to take up half the film. This is not a criticism of the performances of Oliver Reed and Amanda Donohue, who could not have corresponded more precisely to one's mental picture of the characters from Lucy Irvine's book. The dissatisfaction is that, if marriage is the key theme (and Roeg does not appear to use the island for much else), then they did not need to go to Tuin to discover their incompatibility: it is all there in the restaurant scene. The ultimate dramatic problem with *Castaway* – for all the incidental pleasures of the performances, the photography, the score's pleasing pastiches of Debussy – is not that it is about a failed paradise, or a desert island dream that turns into domestic disillusionment. It is that the failure, and the disillusionment, are so predictable.

Track 29 (1987)

A Texan housewife (Theresa Russell) is haunted by the vision of the son she was forced to give up when she was fifteen. Her husband (Christopher Lloyd), a peculiar doctor who is having an affair with a nurse, offers no comfort to the tormented woman.

(*Magills Cinema Annual* 1989[1])

I suppose it's about how we become the persons others want us to be, although we stay the child we originally were. You can become a great brain surgeon or politician – which are intervening titles given to us by others – but immediately the door shuts, out come the model aeroplanes.

(Nicolas Roeg[2])

I've been utterly fed up of being a grown-up for a long time now.

(Martin, played by Gary Oldman, in *Track 29*)

This is a strange black comedy that might ultimately promise more than it delivers but is often funny and always deceptively audacious. The opening is set by Cape Fear River in North Carolina – it will prove a significant setting. A mysterious figure, Martin (Gary Oldman), appears by the roadside, so menacing that a dog barks and then backs off. Is he a ghost, a spirit? One is reminded of the mysterious opening of *The Man Who Fell to Earth*. In the latter film the alien intruder will send shock waves through the entire American

Theresa Russell

117

economy. Martin's impact will be on a more domestic scale, yet still shattering.

The movements of the mystery stranger are crosscut with scenes from the domestic life of Linda Henry (Theresa Russell), which suggests that the two are linked and that their paths are destined to cross. Linda is married to a scatty doctor, Dr Henry Henry (Christopher Lloyd), who works at a geriatric hospital. The marriage seems sexless and Linda desires a child. The idea of children now begins to be prominently established, as well as that of a devitalized marriage. Linda's watching of cartoons and children's programmes like *Superted* on the television, not to mention the brief shot of a doll in her bed, disclose a personality which needs a baby to complete its unfulfilled existence. A grown-up baby will not do. Dr Henry Henry is clearly immature and even his name has overtones of Humbert Humbert in *Lolita*, the man who fell for a nymphette (there is a wide disparity in age between husband and wife). But the childishness of Dr Henry Henry, particularly revealed through his mania for toy trains and the spanking sessions he gleefully undergoes at the hands of Nurse Stein (Sandra Bernhard), suggest warped immaturity more than childlike innocence. Linda's feeling of barren frustration persists.

As the film progresses, Martin seems to move closer to engagement with Linda's dilemma. His difficulty in ordering egg and chips at a café in which Linda is coincidentally present is a neatly played joke at the cultural gap still existing between England and America. Then as Linda and Martin come nearer enigmatic looks are exchanged. Roeg's characteristic shock-cuts slowly reveal themselves as subliminal flashbacks, for Martin's appearance triggers in Linda a memory of a night at a fair-ground, when she was fifteen and brutally seduced by a Martin-lookalike who had the word 'mother' tattooed on his chest. Is Martin the son she later gave birth to, and who was subsequently taken from her? Or is Martin a figure from her subconscious, someone on whom she projects her darkest desires? The trauma of her first sexual encounter, the loss of her baby, a passionless marriage – all these might lead her to summon up an image of Martin, or perhaps project onto the character she meets in the café a hero who will help to 'murder' her husband and help her to escape from the appalling marriage.

Screenwriter Dennis Potter's fascination with childhood can be seen in several of his works, including his TV classic serial, *The Singing Detective*, his screenplay for Gavin Millar's film *Dreamchild*, where an elderly Alice Liddell looks back on her childhood relationship with Lewis Carroll, and his TV play, *Blue Remember'd Hills*, in which adults were dressed as children. As I have said elsewhere[3], one of the main artistic alternatives to the romantic approach to childhood experience has been the Freudian approach, where the artist proposes that the roots of the adult mind and personality are contained in childhood consciousness and experience, with the child's first vision of the sexual act being a crucial formative experience. Because childhood and adulthood in this view are inextricably linked, then the artistic structure demands an interweaving, indeed interlocking, of past and present: Potter's TV screenplay for *The Singing Detective* is a particularly distinguished example of that (as is the Harold Pinter screenplay for Joseph Losey's film of *The Go-Between*). And what does a fascination about childhood reveal? Perhaps a reluctance to grow up. 'I've been utterly fed up of being a grown-up for a long time now', Martin tells Linda, after he has claimed to be her child, and in a sense has come to reclaim a childhood which he feels he has missed.

But might Martin be either a figment of Linda's imagination, or a creature on whom she lavishes a pent-up maternal love because of his physical resemblance to the man who seduced her? He appears at her poolside when she is contemplating suicide after another sexless night with her husband: it is as if she summons the image when she most needs it. A later, apparent conversation with Martin in a café is capped by a superb visual *coup*, when Roeg reveals that Linda is actually sitting on her own. The film's games with fantasy and reality gather momentum towards the close when Martin appears to have inadvertently smashed Henry's lavish train set, only for it to be revealed intact when Henry returns later; or when Henry appears to have been stabbed to death by Martin, only to be seen at the end vainly calling out to Linda as she leaves the house in what seems to be a mood of resolution and finality. Martin is then an imaginative figment who helps Linda to free herself from the trauma of her youth and the barrenness of her marriage. He rescues her just in time.

It should be stressed that Roeg does not make things quite that easy for his audience. As his comment in the epigraph to the film indicates, for him *Track 29* seems as much about identity as it is about childhood, which would particularly link it to films such as *Performance* and *Walkabout*. Childhood is just a dimension of this theme, he suggests, one illustration of the split between the identity that society and other people place on us and what we feel ourselves actually to be and what we secretly desire. This not only involves the mingling of fantasy with reality around Linda and Martin – who are they, really? – but also implicates Dr Henry, who is supposedly a responsible doctor at a geriatric hospital but who undoubtedly feels most himself when he is either being 'admonished' for being a naughty boy by Nurse Stein or when addressing a Trainorama meeting for the miniature train lovers of America. This rouses his enthusiasm to such a degree that it becomes more like a Presidential rally. (It is a deliriously dotty sequence.)

Perhaps of all the cast, Christopher Lloyd as the 'totally loco' Doctor Henry is the one most attuned to the mad humour of the script: he can make a comedy classic even over his character's indecision about the words 'who' and 'whom'. Theresa Russell, once again cast by Roeg as rape victim (as she was in *Bad Timing*) and as someone traumatized by desire for a child (as she was, to some degree, in *Insignificance*), gives a disturbing performance of some neurotic complexity. Gary Oldman as Martin is as boldly repellent here as he was in Alex Cox's *Sid and Nancy* (1986).

As with all Roeg films, *Track 29* is full of curious

quotations, from *Superted* to *Secret Ceremony* (Losey's 1968 film is not alluded to overtly, but the initial plot premise of the Losey film – a young lady following an older lady home before presenting herself to her and calling her her mother has clear affinities with *Track 29*). The most extensive quotation is from J. Lee Thompson's underrated thriller *Cape Fear* (1961), which is on the television as Roeg screws up the tension for a finale in which the Henrys' home is menaced by a night invader; at this point too, composer Stanley Myers does a marvellous Bernard Herrmann pastiche on the soundtrack to parallel the Herrmann score of the older film on TV. Thematically, *Cape Fear* does not appear to have a lot in common with *Track 29*, except that it too has a mysterious intruder whose presence disrupts the marriage of the main couple. But the cross-cutting from the movie on TV to the events in the Henrys' house is undeniably exciting cinema.

The ambience of this situation is, in fact, more Pinteresque than Hollywood thriller: a closed world, as in *The Caretaker* and *Old Times*, into which an intruder enters. He seeks to destroy it but, in that very act of destruction, seems to liberate one of the partners in that world. Perhaps the image which best expresses this liberation is the spreading bloodstain on the ceiling, which seems at first to represent Henry's physical death at the hands of Martin but later seems to represent a more metaphoric death, as Linda psychologically frees herself from a husband now dead to her and appears to embark on a new life. The image recalls the famous image in Hardy's *Tess of the d'Urbervilles* which signals the murder of Alec d'Urberville (the bloodstained ace of hearts on the ceiling) but also the forcible freeing of Tess from all the patriarchal bonds that have tied her.

In an interesting article on the 'family resemblances' in the work of Nicolas Roeg and Dennis Potter, Adam Barker says this about the ending, and other endings in Roeg: 'His films often end with the characters' escape from the claustrophobic confines of the narrative, which is accompanied by their appearance in surprising costume: Tommy in his fedora at the end of *The Man*

Who fell to Earth, Laura (Julie Christie) in widow's weeds on her husband's funeral barge in *Don't Look Now* and Milena transformed into a businesswoman at the end of *Bad Timing*. At the end of *Track 29*, Linda leaves the house smiling, dressed in an immaculate, classical 50s white suit, having spent the rest of the film in 80s housewifely *deshabille*. Even while adhering to the plot's specification of liberating departure, Roeg signals archly that this escape is about as enduring as a change of costume.'[4] Perhaps. Or is the film a reaffirmation of the child in us all? It is a curious affair, a sort of throwback psychodrama that teeters on farce. It has an oddly 60s flavour to it, playing games with fantasy and reality in the manner of *Marienbad* and *Blow-Up*. However, it is not as challenging or as advanced as these films, being more post-modernist than modernist, offering pastiche more than genuine experiment, elusiveness more than genuine enigma and being, in the last resort, unlike the best black comedies, not quite able to take itself seriously. Even Roeg's style here seems in a state of arrested development. Before, his jump cuts and subliminal images sent off sparks of associative ideas, metaphoric connections. Here they are just a fancy way of dressing up flashbacks.

The Witches (1990)

'I'm sure I won't meet one,' I said,
'I sincerely hope you won't,' she said, 'because those
English witches are probably the most vicious in the
whole world.'

(Roald Dahl, *The Witches*)[1]

The author Roald Dahl recently complained with
curmudgeonly vigour to the press about what he
considers improper tampering with his book The
Witches *in the film version just released. In fact, Nicolas*
Roeg's film for which I wrote the screenplay is, with the
exceptions that apparently offend him [the ending has
been changed and Dahl says it is aimed at adults rather
than children], *faithful to the book and its spirit.*

(Allan Scott)[2]

Roeg's reason for doing *The Witches* was that he wanted
to make a film that, for once, his own children could
see. It is his first children's film since *Walkabout*, which,
in commercial terms, tended to fall between two stools
of child and adult appeal. Although not as intricate or
as thematically interesting as the earlier film, *The
Witches* seems to have avoided that particular pitfall; it
has proved one of Roeg's most financially successful
films. It nevertheless provoked the ire of the tale's author,
Roald Dahl, who thought the film 'utterly appalling' and

Anjelica Huston, Bruno Jenkins wished to have his name removed from the credits. It
should be said that Dahl's outburst seemed out of all
proportion to the mild liberties taken by the film.

The Witches is also Roeg's first 'yarn' since *Don't Look Now* and the most linear of his narratives – in other words, his most orthodox, conventional movie. Yet it has its time and place in the cinema of the last decade. It is the last of the gruesome transformation movies of the 1980s, starting with John Landis's *An American Werewolf in London* (1981), moving on to Paul Schrader's *Cat People* (1982), then to Neil Jordan's *The Company of Wolves* (1984), just to name three films with gruesome special effects that turn the human inside out to reveal the monster lurking within. Yet if it is a genial, pint-sized farewell to the 1980s horror film, it might be taken more pointedly as an epitaph for the decade in England as a whole.

The opening is suitably magical. The credits are demonically shaped and in a green-for-danger hue. Stanley Myers's impudent main theme has an edgy effervescence that evokes the great Bernard Herrmann in his fantasy-mode on scores like those for *The Ghost and Mrs Muir* (1947) and *The Three Worlds of Gulliver* (1961). It accompanies a fast travelling shot over snowy landscapes designed to hurl us into a world of fairy tale where fantasy lurks behind the solid houses – the style, colour and atmosphere taking us back almost to the Toytown feel so effectively evoked in the Roeg-photographed *Fahrenheit 451*. Later the ambience of the film will be more earthbound, mundane – Bournemouth. But that in itself will provide the platform for one of Roeg's favourite forms of story-telling: the surreal story in an ostensibly real setting.

'Every country in the world has witches . . . and all have their leader.' The speaker is Helga (Mai Zetterling) a grandma with a stump for a little finger and with a manner that befits a Grimm fairy tale. The awe-stricken listener is her grandson Luke (Jasen Fisher). His name (in the similarity between the words 'Luke' and 'look') seems to betoken alertness: he will *look* for the tell-tale signs of the authentic witch, which include the purple gleam in the eyes, the square-ended toes that demand plain sensible shoes, the bald heads concealed under itchy wigs, and the aversion to the smell of children. To illustrate the danger, Helga tells the story of a girlfriend of her youth, Erica, who was seized by witches. The camera swings nervously as Erica starts to return home with the milk; a black cat crosses her path (a sinister feline will reappear later in the story); she is captured. Later, as her distressed father looks at a painting he has recently acquired (Roeg has mysteriously zoomed towards a lake on the painting in the ominous manner of the opening of *Don't Look Now*), he notices that a figure reminiscent of Erica has appeared where none existed before. The figure moves about on the painting and gradually ages. This idea is not a new one, for M.R. James's classic short story 'The Mezzo-Tint' has a similar situation where a figure appears mysteriously on a painting. But Roeg 'magicks' the material with some visual aplomb. How are we alerted to the fact that the fearsome Miss Ernst (Anjelica Huston) might actually be the Grand High Witch herself? Because when she passes a painting in the hotel lobby and notices a child on the painting, she smiles, pats it with her finger – and the figure disappears.

Dissolve equals disappearance, dissolution in another context. When Luke goes to bed after his parents have gone out of the house, a dissolve from the boy to the unoccupied beds of the adults seems to connote an imminent, ominous absence. Roeg's cockeyed camera-angle for the moment when the parents come out of their house and get into their car also suggests a world out of joint, preparing for the fatal car crash to come. At the same time, it does seem a rather awkward piece of narrative engineering, having no connection with the witches' story, though its placing in the plot seems to suggest that it might have.

The decision to make the boy an American rather than English might have been a strategy designed to make the film appeal more to the American market and, though the part is played well enough by Jasen Fisher, it does seem a little unnecessary. Equally incongruous later is the Grand High Witch's use of the phrase 'candy store', as an explanatory annotation of 'sweet shop' before her assembled audience at the RSPCC

Conference: a minor irritation perhaps but symptomatic of the film's willingness to sacrifice credibility in its desire to reach its audience. It is in that context that Dahl's objection to the changed ending assumes greater importance.

After the death of his parents, Luke is not taken home to America by his grandmother but to his school in England and it is during a game in a tree-house that Luke is first tempted by a witch, a Lady in Black (Anne Lambton) who tries to entice him with a snake, only later having second thoughts and thinking that chocolate might be a more appropriate gift for a young lad. The scene is both funny and frightening. Witch and serpent form a sinuous duo of diabolism, as Luke is almost tempted from the tree of innocence to taste the confectionery of corruption; but the intervention of the grandmother breaks the spell. The Lady in Black departs in high pique, causing the snake also to disappear with, as it were, a petulant sleight of hand. Not all of the subsequent scenes have the same sure lightness of touch, but the ground has been prepared for the confrontation to come between good and evil.

When Grandma is diagnosed as diabetic and a holiday by the sea is recommended, she and Luke go to Bournemouth, Luke taking with him the two white mice Grandma has given him for a birthday present. At the hotel where they are staying, they are harassed by the fussy manager Mr Stringer (Rowan Atkinson), who loathes the idea of pet mice in his hotel and instructs Luke to restrict them to his room. They also become aware of a meeting of the Royal Society for the Prevention of Cruelty to Children (RSPCC), presided over by Miss Ernst. Luke is playing downstairs in the conference room with his mice, which is forbidden, and is trapped as the delegates enter. He has to hide. To his horror, he discovers that the ladies are all witches and that Miss Ernst is the Grand High Witch who plans to turn all the children of England into mice. As a demonstration of her powers, she invites the fat boy, Bruno Jenkins (Charlie Potter), whom Luke has met earlier nibbling at the sandwiches at the buffet, to eat a piece of chocolate injected with her magic Formula 86. He is transformed into a mouse before everyone's eyes. Luke's presence is then scented; a chase ensues; he is caught and he too becomes a mouse.

Several things are interesting about this section of the film. The hotel manager is a traditional figure in the *Fawlty Towers* vein, but he also fleetingly evokes the characterization of the hotel manager in *Don't Look Now*, a man who also disliked his guests and who was also having an affair with one of the hotel maids. *Don't Look Now* is also evoked in the moment when Grandma is having her sandwiches – fish paste suddenly turns to cucumber in her mouth and her tea is dangerously sweetened. She senses something unnerving in the room where they are eating and spots Miss Ernst. Miss Ernst's arrival at the hotel, all sinister shadow, is rather like the filming of George Raft's arrival at the Florida hotel in *Some Like it Hot* (1959) and one wonders whether *The Witches* almost subconsciously picked up on the 'candy' imagery that informs Wilder's film: goodies all around, but something murderous in the cake. Like Spats Columbo in the Wilder film, Bruno is to find that something in the confectionery he is given 'didn't agree with him'. It is a deft touch of adaptation by Allan Scott to introduce Bruno earlier in the film than in the novel, so one can feel a bit more for the character when he is at the mercy of the witches. There is also a nice touch of humour in this scene. During the argument with Mr Stringer about his pet mice, Luke says the hotel probably has mice anyway because the sandwiches have been nibbled. We see Stringer at this reception inspecting the sandwiches for evidence of this, not knowing, of course, that the food *has* been nibbled beforehand by the very human agency of Bruno who, in turn, does not know that his greed is very rapidly going to reduce him to a mouse.

The RSPCC meeting is the longest linear dialogue set piece in any of Roeg's films, longer than anything in, for example, *Insignificance*, which keeps cutting sideways and backwards in time. Roeg clearly thought there was enough incident in the scene not to worry about the static setting. Suspense gathers as some of the ladies begin to scratch their scalps in irritation and their square feet become noticeable. Also, there are to be three shock transformations: the transformation of the imposing Miss Ernst into the gruesome and grotesque Grand High Witch, and the similar processes with the other ladies; the obliteration of one witch who dares to suggest that they cannot possibly wipe out all the children ('Who spoke? Who *dares* to argue with me?' cries the Grand High Witch, her anger instantly translated into *power*); and the reduction of Bruno to a mouse. As Roald Dahl felt, these scenes might be a little frightening for children, though Jim Henson's monsters are not notably more spooky than those he created for, say, *Labyrinth* (1986). And Roeg's quick cutting tends to reduce the gore: it does not have the hideously prolonged effect of the first transformation scene of *The Company of Wolves*, where Little Red Riding Hood seems to have entered the realms of *The Exorcist*. Perhaps the most adult aspect of the scene – and it might only be perceptible to adults as the film attempts to operate on a split level like *Walkabout* – is Anjelica Huston's performance. On the one hand, she has the kind of camp grandeur and cartoon exaggeration that might put her in the tradition of the Queen in *Snow White and the Seven Dwarfs* (1937) or Maleficent in *The Sleeping Beauty* (1959). On the other hand, in her undoubted physical attractiveness and in her seductive approaches to Bruno, there is something more disturbing: it is a performance that expresses the *sensuality* of evil, the allure of the abominable.

'Henceforth we might as well be in Disneyland, where a toe is always kept rooted not so much in reality but in cosy familiarity,' says Tom Milne, talking of the film's shift from the magic of the opening scenes to the mundane mood that permeates the film after the move to England. One problem is the odd clash of acting styles. Mai Zetterling continues with her Grimm characterization, which sits oddly alongside the comic realism of Bill Paterson and Brenda Blethyn as Bruno's parents. Anjelica Huston goes even further than Zetterling into camp caricature and demented fairyland, playing with a pantomime panache, whereas Rowan Atkinson's Mr Stringer seems more like a stand-up routine in search of a sitcom. As for the Disneyfication of Dahl, this was perhaps unavoidable given the children's film ambience and the transformation of mice into heroes. It is a rodent movie in which the resourceful Luke and the everhungry Bruno, still foraging for food in his new mouse guise, begin to look and behave like *The Rescuers*. But at least it recalls the tradition of disquieting, not cute, Disney. The transformation scenes are not as nightmarish as those on Pleasure Island in Disney's *Pinocchio* (1940), for instance, but they do come near to the scarier moments of the British director Jack Clayton's film for the Disney organization, *Something Wicked This Way Comes* (1983): they could give children bad dreams.

What is in the material for Roeg? The narrative structure is straightforward – characters do not go backwards and forwards in their minds as in his other films. Even the special effects, efficient as they are, are no more remarkable than moments in *The Man Who Fell to Earth* or the Professor's vision of a world, a room, a woman in flames at the end of *Insignificance*. Mostly, Roeg seems content to tell the story with a minimum of fuss but with the odd technical flourish: the strategic aerial shot of the conference room to show Luke hiding behind the curtain during the witches' conference; an undulating carpet to show a rodent's progress; point-of-view shots from the perspective of Luke and Bruno Mouse, sometimes even from within the grandmother's handbag; and a dashing moment when Miss Ernst vindictively sends a pram careering towards a cliff edge – at this point Bournemouth beach stands in momentarily for the Odessa Steps, and we are given a sort of seaside postcard version of *Battleship Potemkin*. One incident that is not in the novel but it very well developed in the film concerns a giant black cat on the lookout for Luke, certainly the most fearsome feline since *The Incredible Shrinking Man*. In many ways the film's most striking moment – a wonderful *coup-de-théâtre* – is the moment when the cat hurls itself joyously at full speed through the air towards the hapless Luke Mouse, only to be caught in mid-air by the Grand High Witch herself as she unexpectedly comes back into her room. 'Bad cat, Liebchen,' she purrs, as in thus saving Luke's life, she inadvertently conspires in her own downfall. Even witches are sometimes not the best judges of who their friends really are.

The final part sees the undoing of the witches' plans. Roeg handles nimbly some amusing detail here: Miss Ernst's evident startled discomfiture at Mr Jenkins's casual conversational exchange, 'Just flew in, have you?'; Grandma's unavailing attempt to convince Bruno's parents that the mice in her handbag are not only not as unsanitary as they look but that one of them is actually their son; and farcical events behind the closed doors of the hotel's restaurant, such as the chef's taking revenge on a complaining customer by shovelling disgusting alternatives onto the plate, and Luke's having his tail cut off in the melee following his success in tipping Formula 86 into the witches' soup, or brew. It is Roeg's *The Cook, the Witch, the Mouse and his Grandma* and dispatched with some bravura, if a little unrelenting in its comic mania. The Grand High Witch is cornered and trapped under a water jug: Mr Stringer does the rest with his chopper.

If Roald Dahl hated the ending, where Luke is changed back into human form by the Grand High Witch's ill-used assistant, the reason is that he thought it sentimentalized the story, giving it a 'soppy' denouement. As happy endings go, it seems, in fact, perfectly acceptable, but it is confusingly plotted. Why Luke rushes back into the hotel room when he and his Grandma are on the point of leaving, how they get the witches' money and what they intend to do with it, is not made very clear. Nor is the characterization of the good witch. Are we meant to accept that her change is triggered by resentment against her former mistress when the latter refuses to let her join the ill-fated banquet; or has she been a good witch all along? (It is noticeable that she and her mistress do not speak the same language. 'Lipschen?' she keeps repeating to herself puzzled, as if thinking this is a funny name for a cat.) But then, should this not have been signalled earlier? Or is she still a witch, but just letting Luke and Bruno off the hook, as it were, as the birds seem to be allowing the Brenners to leave their home, even though they could attack them, at the end of Hitchcock's *The Birds* (1963)? Although the ending of *The Witches* is, on the whole, emotionally satisfying, there is still a whiff of red herring and compromise about it, as well as a few perceptible loose structural strings.

Maybe *The Witches* is Roeg's children's version of *Don't Look Now*. This time it is the parents who have been killed, and the bereaved child on holiday in a hotel who is suddenly pursued by the supernatural Furies, or by demonic wicked 'sisters'. One could even take it on a more allegorical level. The witches, who ostensibly live in ordinary houses, work in ordinary shops, might be analogous to Nazi War criminals in hiding (the novel says there are 85 witches in England) and *The Witches*, could be read as a disquieting prophecy of neo-Nazism attempting to take root in England under the guise of a charitable organization: not so much *The Boys from Brazil* as *The Girls from Bournemouth*. Indeed, to put the interpretative frontiers back a little further, could one take *The Witches* as a political allegory of 1980s England? In this reading, the Grand High Witch then becomes Margaret Thatcher, wowing the Bournemouth Conference, not just opposing but *obliterating* dissent, and contriving a future generation made up of mice (like her spineless succession of Cabinet colleagues). She even arrives in Dennis's Taxis.

A children's film? Yes, and no. A political allegory? It's for you to make up your mind. A Nicolas Roeg film? Most certainly – but what does it portend for *his* future?

Conclusion

Is it a coincidence, as I look at my bookshelves, that I see The Probability of the Impossible, The Challenge of Chance, The Roots of Coincidence?

(Nicolas Roeg[1])

Diversity of opinion about a work of art shows that the work is new, complex and vital.
(Oscar Wilde, Preface: *The Picture of Dorian Gray*)

Some bishop said it was obscene and phallic. But that is it isn't *it? That's what it's all about.*
(Nicolas Roeg, on the controversy surrounding his TV commercial on the subject of AIDS[2])

'English – in the teeth of everything,' said D.H. Lawrence, 'even in the teeth of England'. Nicolas Roeg could echo those sentiments. It is not easy being a film-maker in England. Not only are you a prophet without honour in your own country: you are a prophet without profit in your own country. 'What use is a style without a grammar?' Orson Welles used to ask of Michelangelo Antonioni. What use is it being the country's greatest cineaste in a country without a film industry?

Roeg has continued making films against the tide. Think of his record: *Performance* shelved for two years; *Bad Timing* more or less disowned by Rank (they even removed their man with the gong at the start of the picture); *Eureka* withdrawn; *Castaway* delayed and almost foundering until being bailed out by Cannon; and, at time of writing, no sign of Roeg's new film, an adaptation of Brian Moore's *Cold Heaven*. It recalls the wonderful line spoken by Richard Harris in Richard Lester's *Juggernaut* (1974): 'You know what death is, don't you? It's Nature's way of telling you you're in the wrong job'.

What role was found for Roeg during the David Puttnam-inspired jamboree entitled British Film Year in 1985? None. Roeg was not invited to participate, it seems, which would be like celebrating the achievements of the Elizabethan drama without inviting Shakespeare. Admittedly, in Puttnam's words, British Film Year was 'about business, not art', which might explain why a celebratory advertisement in *Screen International* did not include Roeg. (He was, admittedly, excluded in very exclusive company: among others not listed were Lindsay Anderson, Ken Loach, John Boorman, Ken Russell, Jack Clayton, Peter Sasdy, Julie Christie, Michael Radford, Albert Finney and Mike Leigh.) 'It seems that the result of refusing to compromise is that one simply has to survive the best one can,' he said to Brian Baxter at the time[3]. And survivor he is.

Like Blake and Lawrence, Roeg is a particular kind of creative artist whom the English have always found hard to assimilate. He is an English sensualist. He pits a poetic, rich-blooded romanticism against the usual British reserved realism, and a mythical modernism against the more common kitchen-sink naturalism. There is no irony in Roeg, no hiding behind cynicism or deference, or nostalgia. Roeg's films are naked and raw. Because he is outside the mainstream, the making of his films does tend to become a battle. The history of British film seems often to have been an attempt not to nurture but to throttle talent, with an almost perverse inclination to drive its most talented directors abroad.

In fact, Roeg has remained British-based. But there is a curious fact about this home-based director. Of the ten films he has directed, only one has been set exclusively in England. For the rest, he has gone walkabout. This ostensible accident of circumstance has been built into a pervasive theme. His films become about people suddenly away from their roots, losing their physical and moral bearings, floundering in no-man's land. Not knowing *where* they are, they have to find out *who* they are.

In this, as in many other things, they resemble David Lean's films. They too are about mad Englishmen and women going out in the midday sun and losing their heads. What appealed to Roeg about *Castaway*? The sheer *English* eccentricity of the venture: 'If it had been two Americans, they'd have taken pills to turn salt water into fresh water and all kinds of technical stuff. But to arrive with a few boxes and "Did you remember the rice, darling?" "Oh, Christ, I forgot the iodine . . . "'[4] But, more than in Lean, one feels that in Roeg's films this idea is a metaphor for something larger. He likes suddenly taking his characters out of their secure milieu and thrusting them into something strange, unfamiliar and testing, and seeing what reserves they have to cope with the challenge. As he said of *Castaway*: 'They went 12,000 miles to a desert island, but they took themselves. They didn't leave themselves behind.' It follows that such a shake-up of his characters will have consequences for the perceptions of his audience as well.

Roeg is a controversial director who divides, dazzles and dismays audiences and critics. 'There are three lovely critical expressions . . . ' he has said, 'pretentious, gratuitous and profound. None of which I truly understand.'[5] The charge of pretentiousness probably stems from the feeling many people have that his dazzling technique is being thrown away on trivial content. This irritates people more than if ordinary technique were being frittered away on trivial content. Here the gap between ambition and achievement seems frustratingly wide.

Roeg has been increasingly reluctant to talk about his early career as a cameraman. This is probably not so much a desire to denigrate his own past achievements as to discourage a misconception about his subsequent films as a director: that is, the glib critical deduction that, because he was formerly a cameraman, his films have a predictably glittering surface but no depth. Speaking of Josef von Steernberg, John Grierson coined the memorable aphorism: 'When a director dies, he becomes a photographer.' With Roeg, this process seems to have been reversed: when a photographer dies, he becomes a director.

Roeg has fought against this line of logic – 'because I was a cameraman, people tend to look at what I do on the visual level first, and to imagine that the camerawork is primarily in my mind. But I don't think it really is.'[6] (There are, in fact, two misconceptions deriving from Roeg's background: one, that cameramen-turned-directors *necessarily* make visually striking films, which they demonstrably do not; and two, that the essence of Roeg's cinema is in the camerawork, whereas it is in the editing.) Roeg seemed to master the essence of his film language almost instantly, hitting on a style that sometimes seemed a bizarre melange of Hitchcockian montage and Resnais-like mesmerism. ('An amazing film-maker', Roeg has said of Resnais. Like Resnais, Roeg is an obsessive time-traveller in his films.)

Even Pauline Kael acknowledges the bravura brilliance of *Don't Look Now*, but she still dismisses it as 'trash'[7]. Is not such a formidable style wasted on so trite a subject as second sight? But that to some extent depends on whether you think second sight is a trite subject or whether you think it is part of the essence and indeed greatness of cinema that it can endow you, through montage, with the gift yourself. For such a masterfully contrived work, is not the final revelation of a murderous dwarf a severe letdown? But it depends if you wish to take the film on so literal a level: might not the dwarf be a symbolically grotesque transformation of his dead daughter, paying back her guilty father for her death in a setting now less like Venice than Hell itself? 'The first time I saw them [Roeg's films]', said Buck Henry, 'I had a kind of suspended judgement. I didn't know whether they were incredibly pretentious or trying for something so difficult and oblique they just jangled one's ordinary sensibilities of what films are about.'[8]

Roeg is a modernist, and most authentic modernists have had work dismissed as rubbish when it first came out. Roeg is a prickly customer for critics and audiences because, in a Borgesian way, he is probably better at anti-stories than stories. How difficult it must have been for him during the making of *The Man Who Fell to Earth*, as he mediated between a studio head who insisted on a linear narrative and a producer who did not even know what a linear narrative was. Think of the ending of *Bad Timing* and Billie Holliday's song: 'the same old story . . . but it's new to me . . . ' It is the same old story of boy meets girl, but the newness is in the way it is told, moving backwards and forwards in time, unfolding a *lateral* more than a linear narrative. Time is fragmented, perceptions are fractured. Roeg's films often move towards enigma rather than closure, leaving a space that the spectator must fill out for him or herself. 'The film belongs as much to the spectator as to the director', Roeg has said, 'if not more so . . . '[9] Whether, during an era of what Andrew Britton called 'Reaganite entertainment', spectators relished such extra responsibility, having to work at a film's meaning for themselves, is perhaps open to question.

The most contentious area of Roeg's work remains its sexual politics. The most controversial film is still *Bad Timing*, the *Vertigo* of British film (necrophilia, voyeurism, masculine desire and dominance being only some of their common themes). It is assuredly one of the most brilliantly unpleasant films of modern times. Indeed it has been described as a film of 'unpleasure', in which all the seductive values of film – identification with character, transparency of narrative, visual pleasure – have been systematically withheld, in favour of one of the cinema's most fearsome assaults on the audience's eye (and 'I') since Buñuel and Dali. It is Roeg's most searing and Lawrentian dramatization of men and women in conflict (*Castaway* is a pallid palm-tree version of it), of the desire of the male to achieve dominance, of the refusal of the female to accept submission. The problem, or challenge, of the film is to steer a path between a reading in which the woman's punishment for her attempted liberation is seen as tragedy or the film's visual *raison d'être*, and between an interpretation which sees Roeg as a sexual progressive (in his sympathy for the heroine and his unmasking of a masculine monster) or as a misogynistic reactionary, in which the woman properly pays for her permissiveness. Interestingly, the film has been praised in Teresa de Lauretis's feminist book, *Alice Doesn't: Feminism, Semiotics, Cinema* (Macmillan, 1984). It is a film that can be read as an exposure of troubled masculinity, in which Milena – like Sue in *Jude the Obscure* – is a problem for men, not for herself. The unpleasantness of the film does arise from its overwhelmingly masculine point of view, but this has a dual implication. It understandably antagonizes many feminists, but does not the capacity of the film to disturb become an indispensable component of its *critique* of male desire and obsession with domination? Certainly there is an infinite pathos in Milena's last look at Alex, almost like that of the eponymous heroine of James Joyce's story 'Eveline' when her lover calls her name: 'her eyes gave him no sign of love or farewell or recognition.'

Did Art Garfunkel know what he was getting into when he accepted the part of Alex in *Bad Timing*? It is a brave actor who can so unflinchingly cope with so unsympathetic a role. Actors and actresses take big risks when they appear for Roeg. Who would dare be stranded on a desert island with Nic Roeg *and* Oliver Reed? Yet Amanda Donohue has continued to court excitement and danger in her career, as has Theresa Russell: Roeg, as he acknowledges in his praise for the performances in his films of Anita Pallenberg, Jenny Agutter, Julie Christie, Theresa Russell (he would now no doubt add Anjelica Huston), has been singularly blessed with his actresses. Has Donald Sutherland ever been better than in *Don't Look Now*, and has anyone got better performances out of pop stars than Roeg has coaxed out of Jagger and Bowie? The casting of a Roeg film is always weird. Films like *The Man Who Fell to Earth*, *Insignificance* and *Track 29* are essentially fourhanders, but their fascination resides in watching a quartet that is playing on bizarrely different instruments.

In the 1970s, Roeg was described as the director who was keeping the British cinema artistically alive. In the 1980s, there have been hints of a faltering progress or perhaps a pause for second wind. The experience with *Eureka* must have been devastating. Introducing its television screening, Roeg talked of it as a former cripple might who only now is able to walk again. There have been signs since of a certain caution creeping into the style: what Richard Lester has wittily referred to as a director's 'Carl Dreyer period' ('is he still breathing?'). The time-leaps are plumper: *The Witches* really *has* a linear narrative; and the handling of screen time seems both more orthodox and less secure – *Castaway* overstays its welcome, *Track 29* runs out of ideas. But it would be churlish to criticize Roeg for becoming prolific. Film-makers have to earn their living like everyone else. Don Siegel's classic rebuke to the cultists – 'Why didn't you discover me when I was starving?' – is relevant here. Moreover, you do not become a good director by waiting for a great script to come along. As John Ford said, the only way to learn more about directing is by keeping on directing.

Roeg has certainly been an inspiration to others. Collaborators such as writer Paul Mayersberg, cameraman Anthony Richmond, editor Graeme Clifford and writer Terry Johnson have all gone on to try their hands at direction. Mayersberg's *Captive* deserved a wider audience than it found; Richmond's *Déjà Vu*, starring his wife Jaclyn Smith was, alas, something of a disaster; probably the most successful has been Graeme Clifford, notably with his bio-pic of Frances Farmer, *Frances* (1982), which was a controversial piece of movie history but a powerful piece of filmcraft. Outside the mainstream or not, Roeg has been a benevolent influence on British film and a great discoverer of talent. Perhaps remembering his own background, he has not been slow to give a camera operator a considerable leg-up to director of photography. Alex Thomson was Roeg's camera operator when Roeg was photographing *Fahrenheit 451* for Truffaut. He was to become a Roeg cameraman and to help to realize the stunning visuals of *Eureka*.

Roeg's career is at an interesting stage. Unlike that of most English directors of his generation – of any generation, for that matter – it seems to be gathering momentum. He is coming close to averaging a film a year. Can he sustain the freshness of vision? Will he continue to provoke? Encouragingly, even a children's film like *The Witches* managed to outrage somebody – the author of the novel no less. As an inspiration and exhortation to him to continue challenging and harrying a conformist, soporific cinema and a jaded, gullible audience, let me conclude by quoting the words of Dimitri Shostakovich: 'If the production pleases everyone, then consider it a total failure. If, on the other hand, everyone criticizes your piece, then perhaps there's something worthwhile in it. *Real* success comes when people argue about your work, when half the audience is in raptures and the other half is ready to tear you apart.'[10]

By that criterion, Roeg has achieved *real* success commendably often.

Filmography

Films as director

Performance (Great Britain, 1970)

Co-director: Donald Cammell
Producer: Sanford Lieberson; A Goodtimes Production
Screenplay: Donald Cammell
Photography: Nicolas Roeg
Editing: Antony Gibbs
Music: Jack Nitzsche
Production designer: John Clark
Leading players:
James Fox (Chas), Mick Jagger (Turner), Anita
Pallenberg (Pherber), Michele Breton (Lucy), Stanley
Meadows (Rosebloom), John Bindon (Moody), Johnny
Shannon (Harry Flowers), Allen Cutherbertson (Lawyer),
Anthony Valentine (Joey), Kenneth Colley (Tony Farrell),
John Sterland (Chauffeur), Laraine Wickens (Lorraine),
Anthony Morton (Dennis)
Running time: 102 mins.

Walkabout (Great Britain/Australia, 1971)

Producer: Si Litvinoff; Max L. Raub/Si Litvinoff
Production
Screenplay: Edward Bond, based on the novel by James
Vance Marshall (Originally published under the title *The
Children*).
Photography: Nicolas Roeg
Editing: Antony Gibbs and Alan Patillo

Music: John Barry
Production designer: Brian Eatwell
Leading players:
Jenny Agutter (Girl), Lucien John (White boy), David
Gumpilil (Black boy), John Meillon (Father), Peter
Carver (No Hoper), John Illingsworth (Husband), Barry
Donnelly (Australian Scientist), Noelene Brown
(German Scientist), Carlo Manchini (Italian Scientist)
Running time: 100 mins.

Don't Look Now (Britain/Italy, 1973)

Producer: Peter Katz; Casey/Eldorado production
Screenplay: Allan Scott and Chris Bryant. From the short
story by Daphne du Maurier.
Photography: Anthony Richmond
Editing: Graeme Clifford
Music: Pino Donnagio
Production designer: Giovanni Socol
Leading players:
Julie Christie (Laura Baxter), Donald Sutherland (John
Baxter), Hilary Mason (Heather), Clelia Matania
(Wendy), Massimo Serato (Bishop Barbariggo), Renato
Scarpa (Inspector Longhi), Giorgio Trestini (Workman),
Leopold Trieste (Hotel Manager), David Tree (Anthony
Babbage), Ann Rye (Mandy Babbage), Nicholas Salter
(Johnny Baxter), Sharon Williams (Christine Baxter),
Bruno Cattaneo (Detective Sabbione), Adelina Poerio
(Dwarf)
Running time: 110 mins.

The Man Who Fell To Earth (Great Britain, 1976)

Executive Producer: Si Litvinoff
Producers: Michael Deeley and Barry Spikings; British
Lion International
Screenplay: Paul Mayersberg. Based on the novel by
Walter Tevis.
Photography: Anthony Richmond

Editing: Graeme Clifford
Music: John Phillips
Production designer: Brian Eatwell
Leading players:
David Bowie (Thomas Newton), Candy Clark (Mary
Lou), Buck Henry (Farnsworth), Rip Torn (Bryce), Bernie
Casey (Peters), Jackson D. Kane (Professor Canutti), Rick
Ricardo (Trevor), Tony Mascia (Arthur), Linda Hutton
(Elaine), Hilary Holland (Jill), Adrienne Larussa (Helen),
Lilybelle Crawford (Jewellery Store Owner), Richard
Breeding (Receptionist), Albert Nelson (Waiter), Peter
Prouse (Peters' Associate), Capt James Lovell (himself).
Running time: 140 mins.

Bad Timing (Great Britain, 1980)

Producer: Jeremy Thomas; The Recorded Picture
Company
Screenplay: Yale Udoff
Photography: Anthony Richmond
Editing: Tony Lawson
Music: Richard Hartley
Production designer: David Brockhurst
Leading players:
Art Garfunkel (Dr Alex Linden), Theresa Russell
(Milena), Harvey Keitel (Inspector Netusil), Denholm
Elliott (Stefan), Daniel Massey (Foppish man), Dana
Gillespie (Amy), William Hootkins (Colonel Taylor),
Robert Walker (Konrad), Hans Christian (Czech consul),
Sevilla Delofski (Czech receptionist), Ellan Fartt (Ulla),
Nino La Rocca (Arab in truck)
Running time: 123 mins.

Eureka (Great Britain/USA, 1983)

Producer: Jeremy Thomas; Recorded Picture Company
(London)/JF Productions (Los Angeles)
Screenplay: Paul Mayersberg. Based on the book *Who
Killed Sir Harry Oakes?* by Marshall Houts.
Photography: Alex Thomson

Editing: Tony Lawson
Music: Stanley Myers
Production designer: Michael Seymour
Leading players:
Gene Hackman (Jack McCann), Theresa Russell (Tracy), Rutger Hauer (Claude Maillot Van Horn), Jane Lapotaire (Helen McCann), Mickey Rourke (Aurelio D'Amato), Ed Lauter (Charles Perkins), Joe Pesci (Mayakofsky), Helena Kallianotes (Frieda), Cavan Kendall (Pierre de Valois), Corin Redgrave (Worsley), Joe Spinell (Pete), Frank Pesce (Stefano), Michael Scott Addis (Joe), Norman Beaton (Byron Judson), Emrys James (Judge), James Faulkner (Roger), Ann Thornton (Jane), Emma Relph (Mary), Tom Heaton (Man blowing off head).
Running time: 129 mins.

Insignificance (Great Britain, 1985)

Producer: Jeremy Thomas; Zenith Productions. In association with Recorded Picture Company.
Executive Producer: Alexander Stuart
Screenplay: Terry Johnson. Based on his own play.
Photography: Peter Hannan
Editing: Tony Lawson
Music: Stanley Myers, Hans Zimmer
Production designer: David Brockhurst
Leading Players:
Michael Emil (The Professor), Theresa Russell (The Actress), Tony Curtis (The Senator), Gary Busey (The Ballplayer), Will Sampson (Elevator Attendant), Patrick Kilpatrick (Driver), Lou Hirsch (Charlie), Ray Charleson (Bud), Raymond Barry (Ballplayer's father), John Stamford (Young Ballplayer), Desiree Erasmus (Prostitute), David Lambert (Young Professor), Cassie Stuart (Young Actress), Meachell Dunsmoor (Actress as a child), Daniel Benzali (1st Theatrical Agent), RJ Bell (2nd Theatrical Agent), Shinobu Kanai (Japanese Woman), David Montague (Young Senator).
Running time: 109 mins.

Castaway (Great Britain, 1986)

Producer: Rick McCallum; Castaway films. For Cannon.
Executive Producers: Richard Johnson, Peter Shaw
Screenplay: Allan Scott. Based on the book by Lucy
Irvine.
Photography: Harvey Harrison
Editing: Tony Lawson
Music: Stanley Myers, Hans Zimmer
Production design: Andrew Sanders
Leading players:
Oliver Reed (Gerald Kingsland), Amanda Donohue
(Lucy Irvine), Georgina Hale (Sister Saint Margaret),
Frances Barber (Sister Saint Winifred), Tony Rickards
(Jason), Todd Rippon (Rod), John Sessions (Man in pub),
Virginia Hey (Janice), Sorrell Johnson (Lara), Len
Peihopa (Ronald), Paul Reynolds (Mike Kingsland),
Sean Hamilton (Geoffrey Kingsland), Sarah Harper
(Swimming Teacher), Stephen Jenn (Shop Manager),
Joseph Blatchley (Registrar), Simon Dormandy
(Jackson), Ruth Hudson (Receptionist), Gordon
Honeycombe (TV newsreader).
Running time: 120 mins.

Track 29 (Great Britain, 1987)

Producer: Rick McCallum; Hand Made Films
Screenplay: Dennis Potter
Photography: Alex Thomson
Editing: Tony Lawson
Music: Stanley Myers
Production designer: Shuna Harwood
Leading players:
Theresa Russell (Linda Henry), Gary Oldman (Martin),
Christopher Lloyd (Dr Henry Henry), Colleen Camp
(Arlanda), Sandra Bernhard (Nurse Stein), Seymour
Cassel (Dr Bernard Fairmont), Leon Rippy (Trucker),
Vance Colvig (Mr Ennis), Kathryn Tomlinson
(Receptionist), Jerry Rushing (Redneck), Tommy Hull
(Counterman), J. Michael Hunter (Waiter), Richard K.
Olsen (Delegate), Ted Barrow (Old Man).
Running time: 90 mins.

The Witches (USA, 1990)

Executive Producer: Jim Henson
Producer: Mark Shivas; Lorimar Film Entertainment
Screenplay: Allan Scott. Based on the story by Roald Dahl.
Photography: Harvey Harrison
Editing: Tony Lawson
Music: Stanley Myers
Production designer: Voytek, Andrew Sanders
Leading players:
Anjelica Huston (Miss Ernst/Grand High Witch), Mai Zetterling (Helga), Bill Paterson (Mr Jenkins), Brenda Blethyn (Mrs Jenkins), Rowan Atkinson (Mr Stringer), Jasen Fisher (Luke), Charlie Potter (Bruno Jenkins), Anne Lambton (Lady in Black), Jane Horrocks (Miss Irvine), Sukie Smith (Marlene), Rose English (Dora), Jenny Runacre (Elsie), Roberta Taylor (Witch chef), Jim Carter (Head chef)
Running time: 91 mins.

Director of Photography

1961:   *On Information Received* (director: Robert Lynn)
1962:   *Doctor Crippen* (director: Robert Lynn)
1963:   *The Caretaker* (director: Clive Donner)
1964:   *Nothing but the Best* (director: Clive Donner)
1964:   *The Masque of the Red Death* (director: Roger Corman)
1964:   *The System* (director: Michael Winner)
1964:   *Every Day's A Holiday* (director: James Hill)
1966:   *Fahrenheit 451* (director: François Truffaut)
1966:   *A Funny Thing Happened on the Way to the Forum* (director: Richard Lester)
1967:   *Far from the Madding Crowd* (director: John Schlesinger)
1968:   *Petulia* (director: Richard Lester)

Additional Credits

1) With Kevin Kavanagh, Roeg authored the screen-story for the film, *A Prize of Arms* (1961), directed by Cliff Owen.

2) Glastonbury Fayre (1973)

Glastonbury Fayre was filmed during five days in June 1971 at the Glastonbury Festival. Roeg has said that nothing was written down on paper at all. What interested him was not so much the opportunity to film the last of the *Woodstock*-type music festivals as to pick up the associations of Arthurian legend that still clung to aspects of the festival. 'The crowd there interested me', he told Gordon Gow (*Films and Filming*, January 1972), 'because I'd worked on films like *Knights of the Round Table* and *Ivanhoe* [as camera operator] and I never thought they were very well done: they'd just looked up history books and dressed people up, but they didn't behave as if they belonged to the period . . . But at Glastonbury . . . there was the look of a medieval fair to it. They had mummers and jugglers and religious sects. It was a melting pot of human beings, much more than just a show.'

The musical numbers, in their filming, show the influence of Richard Lester, with a bouncy free-ranging montage that recalls Roeg's collaboration with Lester on *A Funny Thing Happened on the way to the Forum*. The hippy, pop-scene ambience has obvious links with *Performance* and indeed seems the kind of occasion from which Mick Jagger's Turner is in retreat. The colour experimentation, with elaborate use of red, blue and yellow filters, is a reminder of the spectacular photographic effects Roeg achieved for Roger Corman's *The Masque of the Red Death*. Characteristic Roeg tics abound: startling imagery (the stage as pyramid, the obsession with perception and vision); elaborate intercutting (between contrasting religious services, for instance); the atmosphere of sensuality, ecstasy, Lawrentian release (a bracing roll in the mud). The performers, who include Hawkwind, Melanie and

Fairport Convention are relatively unmemorable, but the filming is constantly quirky and lively – a sunny, orgiastic, eerie relic of a bygone period. The direction is credited to Peter Neal, and Roeg is included among the other cameramen such as Tony Richmond (soon to become Roeg's regular cameraman) and Mike Molloy. David Puttnam is listed as one of the producers. The film was released in 1973.

3) Aria (1987)

Aria, produced by Don Boyd, was a film in which ten directors, were invited to make a short film based on an operatic aria of their choice. In addition to Roeg, the directors were Robert Altman, Bruce Beresford, Bill Bryden, Jean-Luc Godard, Derek Jarman, Franc Roddam, Ken Russell, Charles Sturridge and Julien Temple.

Roeg's segment, which appeared first in the film, is inspired by an aria from Verdi's *A Masked Ball – Un Ballo in Maschera*. The opera was inspired by the assassination of King Gustav III of Sweden at a masked ball in 1792. However, Roeg has used the music to accompany a bizarre recreation of the attempted assassination of King Zog of Albania in 1931 as he was on his way to the Vienna Opera House, an attempt foiled when, uniquely in the annals of royal assassination attempts, the monarch started firing back.

Roeg was toying with the idea of casting Jeremy Irons in the role of King Zog, with Theresa Russell as his mistress, but, in a wild moment, Don Boyd suggested that Theresa Russell play the role of the monarch, and both she and Roeg were much taken with the idea. It is a strikingly shot segment, with deft use of cross-cutting and elaborate zooms, and Roeg takes the operatic context as a cue to direct the film in the stylized form of silent film melodrama. 'King Zog shot back!' says an inter-title. Theresa Russell's masculine performance is very effective, and the moment when the shooting starts and the masks are ripped off faces is a real *coup de théâtre*. The use of masks, and the female playing the male lead, are aspects which one could relate to characteristics elsewhere in Roeg, notably his fascination with the ambiguity of identity and the fluidity of gender, from *Performance* onwards.

On a domestic note, the film was a real family affair: his wife, Theresa Russell in the leading role; eldest son Waldo as first assistant director; Nico Roeg as unit stills photographer; Luc Roeg (who played the boy in *Walkabout*) as associate producer, and Sholto Roeg as the production runner. The 18-month-old Max Roeg had a cameo role as the Baroness's son, and the two dogs were played by the family German shepherd dogs, Jessie and Annie. The film was photographed by Harvey Harrison.

Select
Bibliography

Interviews

Baxter, Brian

'The Significance of Mr Roeg', *Films and Filming*, July 1985, pp. 14–17.

Gow, Gordon

'Identity: an interview with Nicolas Roeg', *Films and Filming*. January, 1972, pp. 18–25.

Milne, Tom and Houston, Penelope

'Don't Look Now: Interview with Nicolas Roeg', *Sight and Sound*, Winter 1973/4, pp. 2–8.

Roddick, Nick

'None of the Above: Nicolas Roeg', *Cinema Papers*, Issue 53: September 1985, pp. 41–4.

Books

Feineman, Neil

Nicolas Roeg, Boston: Twayne Publishers, 1978.

Norman, Neil and Barraclough, John

Insignificance: the Book, Sidgwick and Jackson, 1985. (Foreword by Nicolas Roeg: including the screenplay by Terry Johnson).

Articles

Barker, Adam	'What the Detective Saw: Dennis Potter and Nicolas Roeg', *Monthly Film Bulletin*, May 1988, pp. 195–7.
Crawley, Tony	'The Last British Film-maker', *Films Illustrated*, July 1980, pp. 391–6.
Dawson, Jan	'*Bad Timing*', *Cinema Papers*, August-September, 1981, pp. 227–30.
Dempsey, Michael	'*Don't Look Now*', *Film Quarterly*, Spring 1974, pp. 39-43.
Farber, Stephen	'*Don't Look Now*', *New York Times*, December 23, 1973, p. 15.
Gussow, Mel	'Roeg: The Man Behind *The Man Who Fell to Earth*', *New York Times*, August 22, 1976, p. 12.
Izod, John	'*Walkabout*: A Wasted Journey?' *Sight and Sound*, Spring 1980, pp. 113–116.
Kael, Pauline	'The Current Cinema: *Don't Look Now*', *New Yorker*, December 24, 1973, pp. 68–70.
Kinder, Marsha and Houston, Beverle	'Seeing is Believing: *The Exorcist* and *Don't Look Now*', *Cinema*, Issue No. 34, 1974, pp. 22–33.
Kolker, Robert Phillip	'The Open Texts of Nicolas Roeg', *Sight and Sound*, Spring 1977, pp. 82–4.

Mayersberg, Paul	'The Story So Far . . . *The Man Who Fell to Earth*', *Sight and Sound*, Autumn 1975, pp. 225–31.
Milne, Tom	'*The Man Who Fell to Earth*', *Sight and Sound*, Summer 1976, pp. 145–7.
Petley, Julian	'*Performance*', *The Movie*, No. 90, 1981, pp. 1796–7.
Sinyard, Neil	'British Film Since the Second World War', *The Cambridge Guide to the Arts in Great Britain, Volume 9*, edited by Boris Ford, Cambridge University Press, 1988, pp. 238–51.
Walker, Alexander	'No Sympathy for the Devil', *Hollywood UK – The British Film Industry in the Sixties*, New York 1976, pp. 416–425.
Wright, Basil	*The Long View*, St. Albans Press, 1976, pp. 572–5.

The Films of Nicolas Roeg

Notes

Introduction

1 *Hitchcock by Francois Truffaut*, Secker & Warburg, 1966, p. 100.
2 'Identity: Nicolas Roeg in an interview with Gordon Gow', *Films and Filming*, January 1972, p. 19.
3 'None of the Above', *Cinema Papers*, Issue No. 53, September 1985, p. 43.
4 'How Roeg Struck Gold in Hollywood: an interview with Christopher Keats', *The Guardian*, July 1, 1982, p. 11.
5 Quoted in James Park's *Learning to Dream*, Faber 1984, p. 50.
6 *Cinema Papers*, September 1985, p. 43.
7 *Films and Filming*, January 1972, p. 21. See also the tribute that Roeg paid to Truffaut in 'Looking at the Rubber Duck': Nicolas Roeg talks to Richard Combs about *Fahrenheit 451*' in *Sight and Sound*, Winter 1984/5, pp. 43–4.

Performance

1, 2 Both quoted in Leslie Halliwell's *Film Guide*, 1989 edition, Granada, 1989.
3 David Shipman's *The Story of Cinema: Volume 2* (Hodder & Stoughton, 1985) makes one slighting reference to *Performance*, grouping it alongside

another half-a-dozen Warners' movies that the public did not want to see. Patricia Warren's picture history of British Film to celebrate British Film Year, *The British Film Collection, 1896–1984* (Elm Tree Books, 1985) makes no reference to *Performance* at all. Another standard history, George Perry's *The Great British Picture Show* (Paladin 1975) makes one rather puzzled reference to *Performance* – 'a bewildering film, partly because of its deliberate attempt to confuse identities. The pop singer and the gangster see in each other an alternative version of themselves, an effect accentuated when even their appearances are swapped' (p. 276). Having proceeded this far, Perry obviously feels it wiser to go no further. Alternatively, Basil Wright in his film history, *The Long View* (St Albans Press, 1976) proffers a more thoughtful, detailed reading, whilst Roy Armes's *A Critical History of the British Cinema* (Secker & Warburg 1978) affords the film the compliment of having a still from *Performance* as its cover illustration.

4 Quoted in Leslie Halliwell's *Film Guide*, 1989.
5 'Don't Look Now: Nicolas Roeg interviewed by Tom Milne and Penelope Houston', *Sight and Sound*, Winter 1973/4, p. 7.
6 This might be anticipated by that strange shot of the back of someone's head just before Chas shoots Joey: the head, as we realise afterwards, is Turner's.
7 For example, the shot of Chas's back, that still bears the scars of his earlier beating, reveals to Turner and his girlfriend evidence of Chas's gangster background.
8 '*Performance* was really a fifty-fifty collaboration', said Roeg (*Films and Filming*, January 1972, p. 22). 'I wouldn't take credit for more than fifty-per-cent of the movie, and I know Donald [Cammell] wouldn't either'. Perhaps this is the place to indicate what one is implying when one talks of a 'Nicolas Roeg movie'. Here I wish to borrow the formulation of Philip Kemp in his splendid new book on Alexander Mackendrick, *Lethal Innocence* (Methuen, 1990): 'This is perhaps the place to make the standard disclaimer which, in a post-auteurist era, any study of a director must include.

References to "Mackendrick's films" or "Mackendrick's work" may seem to imply that he was the sole author of his movies. No such suggestion, of course, is intended – as Mackendrick himself, who dislikes "the utterly unjustified cult of the director" would be the first to insist. Such phrases are shorthand, to avoid cumbersome repetition . . . At the same time, though, it's possible to argue, as V.F. Perkins does in *Film as Film* that "the director is the only member of the production team who can see (whose job it is to see) the whole film rather than particular aspects, the interrelationship of the parts rather than the parts as separate tasks". (p. xi) I would endorse that and my usage of a phrase like 'Roeg's work' or 'Roeg's films' contains all the implications, qualifications and modifications that Kemp outlines in his approach to Mackendrick.

9 Malcolm Bradbury and Ian McFarlane, (editors), *Modernism* (Penguin 1976), p. 51.

Walkabout

1 James Vance Marshall, *Walkabout*, Penguin 1979, p. 25.
2 *Sight and Sound*, Winter 73/4, p. 7.
3 'The Significance of Mr Roeg: interview with Brian Baxter', *Films and Filming*, July 1985, p. 15.
4 Neil Feineman, *Nicolas Roeg*, Twayne Publishers, 1978, pp. 61–83.
5 Basil Wright, *The Long View*, pp. 571–5.
6 John Izod, '*Walkabout*: A Wasted Journey?', *Sight and Sound*, Spring 1980, pp. 113–16.
7 *Films and Filming*, January 1972, pp. 22–3.
8 D.H. Lawrence, 'A Study of Thomas Hardy', *Selected Literary Criticism of D.H. Lawrence*, (Heinemann Educational Books, 1967), pp. 176–7.
9 As Basil Wright has put it: 'When in this film Roeg brings us up against a brick wall, the result is not only abrasive, it is concussive; because behind the wall, as we see, are two desolations, not one – the

desolation of the city and the desolation of the desert'. (*The Long View*, p. 573).

10 Robin Wood, *The American Nightmare*, Festival of Festivals: Toronto, 1979, p. 49.

11 The novel was originally published in 1959 by Michael Joseph under the title of *The Children*.

12 John Izod has discussed the significance of their Englishness interestingly in his *Sight and Sound* article, mentioned earlier: 'A number of hints (the family describe themselves as English, Housman's verse; Roeg's own nationality) suggest that the Australian plot might conceal a parable for England. And England's stagnation is a more familiar theme than Australia's' (p. 116).

13 James Vance Marshall, *Walkabout*, pp. 25–6.

14 Roy Armes, *A Critical History of the British Cinema*, p. 320.

15 *Sight and Sound*, Spring 1980, p. 116. Although the ending of *Walkabout* is far from sentimental, it is arguable whether the Housman quotation is really necessary. Is it redundantly reinforcing in verbal form what Roeg has implicitly and subtly already conveyed in visual terms? Still, it is not the only Roeg film to end this way: *Eureka* also has a literary epitaph, from the Robert Service poem, 'Spell of Yukon'. Also my doubts about this ending were somewhat assuaged when, after a screening of the film on television, I was telephoned by an ex-student who had been deeply moved by the film and wished to know the source of the poem which, for him, completed the film in a very satisfactory way and brought its themes into stark focus.

16 See *Films Illustrated*, November 1976. Peter Weir elaborated on his admiration for Roeg in a *Cinema Papers* interview (September-October 1981, p. 327) when he was asked if he had considered any kind of similarity between his work and Roeg's: 'I have loved a number of his films and, yes, there are areas where our paths have crossed. But in other areas we diverge. His treatment of sexuality or sex is different from mine or more predominant. He uses that as part of his tension. I use other systems. It's like waving at

someone in the distance and sharing a smile. But that's about as much as I know about him'.

Don't Look Now

1 *Sight and Sound*, Winter 1973/4, p. 3.
2 S.S. Prawer has commented on the 'vivid colour scheme of *Don't Look Now* – with its sinister incursions of red' – in *Caligari's Children* (Oxford, 1980, pp. 216–17). In a stimulating commentary, Prawer finds it 'particularly apt because the film's central protagonist is an art-historian, a man professionally concerned with the meaning of colour gradations' and links it to the horror film's characteristic use of the emotional effect of colour (Hitchcock, too, one might add parenthetically, is especially good at this). D.G. Winston's phrase for this, he notes, is 'non-verbal thought': 'thought that does not first appear in our minds in the form of words, and is therefore inadequately expressed by them – thoughts that are more often associated with colour, composition and mood than with syntax and logic'.
3 R.P. Kolker, *The Altering Eye*, Oxford 1983, p. 221.
4 *Sight and Sound*, Winter 1973/4, p. 4.
5 *Films and Filming*, November 1973, p. 45.
6 Quoted in Harry T. Moore's biography of Lawrence, *The Priest of Love* (Heinemann, 1974), p. 328.
7 D.H. Lawrence, *England, my England*, Penguin 1960, p. 39. Lawrence said of the central character: 'The hero of my story is a spiritual coward. But then, who isn't?' Would Roeg say the same of John Baxter in *Don't Look Now*?
8 *Cinema*, Issue No. 34, Spring 1974, p. 33.
9 Walter Tevis, *The Man Who Fell to Earth*, Abacus, 1988, pp. 102–3.

The Man Who Fell to Earth

1 Walter Tevis, *The Man Who Fell to Earth*, Abacus 1988, p. 104. (The novel was first published in 1963).

2 Quoted in Alexander Walker's splendid book, *National Heroes: British Cinema in the Seventies and Eighties*, Harrap 1985, pp. 139–40.
3 *Sight and Sound*, Summer 1976, p. 198.
4 *Monthly Film Bulletin*, April 1976, p. 86.
5 Tevis, *The Man Who Fell to Earth*, p. 146.
6 R.P. Kolker, 'The Open Texts of Nicholas Roeg', *Sight and Sound*, Spring 1977, pp. 82–4.
7 Walker, *National Heroes*, p. 138.
8 Roeg would not have been the first to use Icarus as a symbol of the artist, always in danger of flying too near the sun in his over ambitiousness. Think of James Joyce's use of the same image in *A Portrait of the Artist as a Young Man*, or, for that matter, Woody Allen in *Stardust Memories*. But, as Robert Browning would say, a man's reach must exceed his grasp, or what's a Heaven for? It is in a sense, the *duty* of the artist to over-reach himself, to take risks, and the responsibility of the critic to respect that endeavour.
9 Paul Mayersberg, 'The Story so far . . . ', *Sight and Sound*, Autumn 1975, p. 226.

Bad Timing

1 *Films and Filming*, July 1985, p. 16.
2 Quoted in James Park's *Learning to Dream* (Faber, 1984), p. 119.
3 *Sir Thomas Beecham*, by Neville Cardus, Collins, 1961, p. 115.
4 *Films Illustrated*, July 1980, p. 392.
5 Allessandra Comini, *Gustav Klint*, Thames and Hudson, 1975, pp. 5–6.
6 Jan Dawson, 'Bad Timing', *Cinema Papers*, August-September 1980, p. 228.
7 D.H. Lawrence, *Women in Love* (Penguin, 1960), p. 498. Lawrence's bafflement over Gudrun is not dissimilar to Alex's over Milena: 'What was it, after all, that a woman wanted? Was it mere social effect, fulfilment of ambition in the social world, in the community of mankind? Was it even a union in love

and goodness? Did she want "goodness"? Who but a fool would accept this of Gudrun? This was but the street view of her wants. Cross the threshold and you found her completely, completely cynical about the social world at its advantages. Once inside the house of her soul, and there was a pungent atmosphere of corrosion, an inflamed darkness of sensation, and a vivid subtle, critical consciousness that saw the world distorted, horrific'. (pp. 507–8). In both *Bad Timing* and *Women in Love*, there is the same fusion of love and death in their central relationships, where obsession seems to lead inexorably to destruction. 'The moment he [Gerald] saw Gudrun something jolted in his soul', Lawrence writes. 'She was looking rather lofty and superb, smiling slowly and graciously to the Germans. A sudden desire leapt in his heart to kill her. He thought, what a perfect voluptuous fulfilment it would be to kill her'. (p. 518). Alex's desire to possess Milena completely will also amount finally to a desire to kill her, or at least possess her finally in death.

8　John Pym, 'Ungratified Desire: Nicolas Roeg's *Bad Timing*', *Sight and Sound*, Spring 1980, p. 112.
9　*Cinema Papers*, August-September 1980, p. 228.
10　*Films Illustrated*, July 1980, p. 393.
11　*Cinema Papers*, August-September 1980, p. 228.

Eureka

1　Paul Mayersberg, *Sight and Sound*, Autumn 1982, p. 282.
2　*The Guardian*, July 1, 1982, p. 11.
3　Ibid.
4　Giuseppe di Lampedusa, *the Leopard*, (Collins 1961), p. 59.
5　*Monthly Film Bulletin*, May 1983, p. 119.
6　John Boorman, *Money into Light*, Faber 1985, p. 67.

Insignificance

1 From *Insignificance: The Book* (Sidgwick and Jackson Ltd., 1985) by Neil Norman and Jon Barraclough. Foreword by Nicolas Roeg, p. 1.
2 'Relatively Speaking', *Monthly Film Bulletin*, August 1985, p. 237.
3 'Backwards into the Myths', *The Guardian* 8 August, 1985, p. 9.
4 *Monthly Film Bulletin*, August 1985, p. 237.
5 Ibid., p. 238.
6 *Insignificance: The Book*, p. 123.

Castaway

1 Derek Malcolm, 'Lust at Sea', *The Guardian*, February 19, 1987, p. 11.
2 Philip French, *The Observer*, February 22, 1987, p. 27.
3 Pam Cook, *Monthly Film Bulletin*, February 1987, p. 42.
4 *Films and Filming*, July 1985, p. 14.
5 *The Observer*, February 22, 1987, p. 27.
6 *Sight and Sound*, Winter 1973/4, p. 3.
7 *Channel 4 TV programme guide*, November 24–30, 1990.

Track 29

1 *Magills Cinema Annual 1989* (Salem Press: Los Angeles, 1988), p. 436.
2 *The Listener*, May 26, 1988, p. 13.
3 The argument is developed in my book, *Childhood in the Movies*, (Batsford: forthcoming 1992).
4 'What the Detective Saw', *Monthly Film Bulletin*, May 1988, p. 195.

The Witches

1 Roald Dahl, *The Witches*, Puffin, 1985, p. 35.
2 Allan Scott, *The Guardian*, July 25, 1990, p. 27.

Conclusion

1 *Insignificance: The Book*, p. 1.
2 *Time Out*, February 18–25, 1987, p. 22.
3 *Films and Filming*, July 1985, p. 16.
4 *Time Out*, February 18–25, 1987, p. 22.
5 *Films Illustrated*, July 1980, p. 393.
6 *Films and Filming*, January 1972, p. 18.
7 Pauline Kael, *Reeling*, Warner Books, 1976, p. 323.
8 'The Last British Film-Maker', *Films Illustrated*, July 1980, p. 391.
9 See the interview with Gordon Gow, *Films and Filming*, January 1972, p. 21.
10 *Testimony: The Memoirs of Dmitri Shostakovich*, as related to and edited by Solomon Volkov, Faber 1981, p. 82.

Index